HEALTHY BODY, PEACEFUL MIND, AWAKENED SPIRIT.

A Review of Selected Aspects of Body, Mind, and Spirit Well-being

HELEN BIRNBAUM

BALBOA.
PRESS

A DIVISION OF HAY HOUSE

Scripture quotations marked TLB are taken from The Living Bible copyright © 1971. Used by permission of Tyndale House Publishers, Inc., Carol Stream, Illinois 60188. All rights reserved.

Balboa Press books may be ordered through booksellers or by contacting:

Balboa Press
A Division of Hay House
1663 Liberty Drive
Bloomington, IN 47403
www.balboapress.com
1 (877) 407-4847

Print information available on the last page.

ISBN: 978-1-5043-8170-3 (sc)
ISBN: 978-1-5043-8171-0 (hc)
ISBN: 978-1-5043-8172-7 (e)

Library of Congress Control Number: 2017908636

Balboa Press rev. date: 06/15/2017

To my children, Dana and David, with love.

Thankfully, you survived less-than-perfect parenting and have matured into extraordinary adults that I am truly proud of.

To my brother Tommy. I feel a special closeness to you despite the huge physical distance between us. Thank you for being there for me always.

To the memory of my parents. Only now do I fully appreciate how exceptionally caring they were. Their integrity and wisdom laid a solid foundation that has sustained me throughout my life.

Contents

Introduction

For years I have been interested in the body-mind-spirit connection and the holistic approach to health. I have read widely and received training in many alternative healing techniques, namely reflexology, Reiki, Bach flower therapy, educational kinesiology, and EFT. These therapies embrace holistic principles and treat the whole person (not isolated parts), taking into account the emotional condition of the person as well.

My initial motivation for writing this book was to bring together and share the information I had accumulated in the above-mentioned healing modalities and to explain how they work. However, since I believe that we have a great need for spiritual connection and that without it our level of well-being cannot reach its full potential, the book gradually evolved to include spirituality and mysticism as well.

Since this book is in essence a review, it embraces the knowledge and wisdom of many authors and experts. Every source that I quote is listed in the bibliography at the end of the book. The authors mentioned in the text are listed there in alphabetical order. A reader who wishes to delve more deeply into a particular subject can easily access the relevant references. Throughout the book I present my own insights and conclusions as I describe my personal life experiences and my journey of discovery.

The book is divided into four parts. The first three, "Physical Well-being," "Mental Well-being," and "Spiritual Well-being," may be read in any order. I believe that to be a balanced human being, one needs to pay attention to all three aspects of well-being. If one of these is off-kilter, we are not able to live our best possible lives. The last part, "The Bigger Picture," deals with new discoveries in science and how the convergence of science and spirituality is enhancing our understanding of the world beyond our visible three-dimensional existence. This last part weaves together the information and concepts in parts 1 through 3 to give a final tapestry that shows the greater picture.

The knowledge I have accumulated from my study and training has helped me to reach a level of well-being that I am happy with—a healthy body, inner peace, and contentment most of the time.

Of course, there are many for whom this knowledge is already an integral part of their lives and work, and for these people this book may not be of interest. My aim is to reach those who have not yet discovered this information for themselves, either because they have not been exposed to it or have chosen to disregard it as nonsense. There are many people who reject the concepts presented here, claiming that there is no scientific evidence for them. For the latter especially, I provide logical explanations and scientific proof where possible.

My wish is that the information in this book will arouse in the reader an interest in the body-mind-spirit continuum, which in essence is what we are. Awareness of the role that spirituality plays in our lives provides an understanding of the tremendous resource we have within us and allows us to optimize our personal potential.

The wealth of knowledge that is available today impacts our lives as never before, in ways that can be immensely empowering. May you find and develop your own personal power so that you can live the life you desire.

Note

To avoid the cumbersome use of both genders (he/she and his/hers), I use the masculine pronouns only. This in no way implies superiority of the male sex. It is merely for convenience.

My Own Journey

I was blessed with a normal and mostly happy childhood that was free of major traumatic experiences. When I look back, I understand that I was also blessed with wonderful, caring parents, although this was not always obvious to me, especially during my teens.

My family lived modestly but comfortably. I attended a private girls' school where I was very happy, and then studied biology at university. My first job after obtaining a B.Sc. (Honors) was at the South African Institute for Medical Research. During my first year there, I met someone who swept me off my feet. We got married, and I moved to a neighboring country where he lived. After three years we returned to my beloved South Africa, which I missed so much. I continued my studies in plant sciences at my alma mater, and I was granted an M. Sc. (*cum laude*). I continued to do research toward a Ph.D. and was offered the position of lecturer in plant physiology. At about this time, my marriage ended in divorce after eleven years and thankfully, no children. (At that time, being a single mother would have been very challenging.)

My late twenties and early thirties were quite stormy at the behavioral and emotional levels. I was more or less a practicing Catholic, but the weekly Sunday rituals and formal rote prayers had become meaningless to me. My faith was not providing the soul food that I needed at that time. Next to the university where

I worked, there was a little church that I would go to occasionally for quiet contemplation. I was looking for inner peace or whatever was missing that I craved. I sat there many times but didn't find whatever it was that I needed. By this time I was already disillusioned with the narrow view of my religion and its arrogant intolerance of other faiths. For instance, it made no sense to me that I couldn't take communion at the interfaith meetings held at the university because they were run by a Methodist minister and I was Catholic. This attitude upset me. After all, if we all worship the same God, what does it matter if we participate in a ceremony of a different tradition? At the time I was still unaware of the political side of most orthodox religions and therefore had not yet developed a cynical attitude toward them.

In my mid-thirties I fell in love with a fellow biologist who was in the same field of research. We married and moved to Israel, where my life changed completely in every way, overnight. Almost immediately, I began to learn about Judaism, and converted two years later. I also had to study Hebrew, which I found very difficult. Although I understood the spoken language, I was incapable of putting together a sentence without mistakes. It remained a challenge for many years. Now after repeated efforts and with the aid of a technique that I learned recently, I feel I have finally mastered the language. After two years of being in Israel, my daughter was born. Shortly afterward, we had a sabbatical abroad, and then my son was born. Moving from country to country meant that I had no close friends or family nearby. At that stage I did not 'mix' very easily socially. Besides being shy, my background was totally incongruous with my new reality, and the language barrier didn't help. In a way I remained an outsider. Life was not easy, but it was bearable. Through my marriage I did gain a warm, loving family in Israel, and for this I am most appreciative and grateful. The local people I met were wonderful, and although they were accepting, I clearly was not 'one of them'. I take some responsibility for this as I am quite a loner and did not really try to fit in. Books became my companions, and I read extensively. I must add that today my situation is entirely different. After losing my husband to cancer, I discovered the treasure of friendship as I lived through some tough times. The few friends I had, especially those at work, stood by me through it all in a way I will never forget. I cherish these lovely people to this day.

When my children were young, I often wondered how to use hands-on healing to relieve them of minor illnesses or discomfort. Then one day on a free afternoon (a very rare treat for me in those days), I chanced upon a delightful little bookshop in Jerusalem. One of my favorite pastimes is browsing in bookshops, so finding this treasure of English books was better than winning a million dollars (or almost better). I bought two books by Barbara Brenner about hands-on healing. They were intense and beyond me, but I learned interesting things about the aura. (Brennan is a psychotherapist and scientist apart from being an energy healer). I also found a lovely book on Reiki with beautiful pictures and good explanations titled *The Power of Reiki* by Tanmaya Honervogt. It was just what I needed as it taught me about hands-on healing. I was hooked.

I received training in the Reiki I and Reiki II degrees shortly afterward, followed by a course on reflexology sometime later. Over the following years, I learned kinesiology, Bach flower therapy, EFT, and dowsing.

I tend to think of the Reiki one course as the beginning of my journey into the world of energy healing and connection to Spirit. However, the *connection* was already in place in early childhood, and since my early twenties I have been drawn to books about mysticism and the supernatural. Although I have a background in the sciences (mainly biology, with a healthy dose of chemistry and biochemistry), my curiosity and acceptance of the paranormal have led me to explore, through reading, the vast and amazing world beyond the physical, the one that is invisible to our human perceptions.

Recently, a friend asked me, "What makes you a specialist on well-being to write a book about it?" This is a question that no one had asked me before, and it gave me pause. Maybe other friends had the same thought but were too polite to voice it? After considering my own excellent state of well-being, fifty years of regular exercise, my background in biology and chemistry, my knowledge of how the body functions, and my long-held interest and training in holistic therapies, I decided that yes, I am qualified to review the subject and to share it. It may be argued that I owe my state of well-being to my lucky genetic makeup. I had relatively healthy parents who lived to the ripe age of ninety-plus. I believe that their good health was in large part due to wholesome nutrition. In those days milk came in glass bottles. Cattle roamed the meadows and fed on grass rather than chemical-laden grains, and our homegrown chickens ran around freely, happily scratching around for their between-meal snacks. My father grew many kinds of fruits and vegetables on natural compost-rich soil, and these went straight from the garden to the table.

Since leaving home (almost half a century ago), I have been consuming the factory-farm meat and commercially available fruits and vegetables like everyone else. I have been fortunate to stay healthy despite some bad habits, such as too much coffee and sugar (the consequences of which are mentioned in the text). But most of all, the likely reason for my state of well-being may be my positive mental attitude toward health, and my spiritual beliefs. However, I do not live in fairyland. I do get ill, and I stress out occasionally. But focusing on the things that promote good health rather than worrying about getting sick is an approach that matches what scientist and author Bruce Lipton discovered about the effect of the environment (both external and internal) on the activity of our genes. He explains how our minds and beliefs determine the environment of our cells and thus our physiology. His book *The Biology of Belief* is a forerunner in the new science of Epigenetics, which teaches that we are not passive victims of our genetic heredity as was previously accepted. We can control our internal cellular environment through wholesome thoughts and beliefs, and thus, achieve and maintain excellent health.

Since I have personally gained so much from the knowledge that I have accumulated over the years, I feel compelled to share it in this book with whoever may be interested. I invite you to explore this treasure trove of sound knowledge that uplifts and empowers. My personal journey has brought me from being inhibited, uncomfortable in my own skin, and joyless to feeling self-confident, free, and appreciative of life's many gifts. I have learned to avoid the issues and behaviors that sap my peace of mind, and I am more aware of how easily misunderstandings arise and dramas develop. Now I can say that I have grown into the person I have always wanted to be. This change in mind-set was gradual, and I owe it partly to the many authors who have made available their knowledge and experience of healing, growth, and self-empowerment. I condense the information on *physical, mental, and spiritual well-being* from these sources, all of which are acknowledged and fully cited, as well as my own personal experience and understanding.

I hope that this book shows you ways of achieving balance in body, mind, and spirit and helps you to find inner peace and meaning in your life.

Part 1

Physical Well-being

Chapter 1

Commonsense Health and Some Things You May Not Know

If you want to be healthy in body and mind, then *move*! Voluntary movement characterizes all living members of the animal kingdom.

Couch potatoes are living beings, but barely so. It is a known fact that exercise is good for us, but so many of us leave it out of our to-do lists. Our modern lifestyles make it inevitable that we spend most of our days sitting at our desks, commuting, and chilling out in front of the television. The consequences are obvious—excess weight, tiredness, stiff joints, and sluggish metabolism. By the end of a long workday, most of us just want to relax—and the only moving we end up doing is from couch to refrigerator and back again. You don't need to join a club or spend a lot of money. Just add walking to your daily schedule. It is not as easy as it sounds, I know. I usually don't walk unless I have to. For instance, I walk the dog when I am the only one who is home and the dog needs to be walked. (What a drag!) It's a matter of putting *walk* in your schedule and getting used to it. To my surprise, I found that I actually missed walking the dog when my son moved out to a place of his own and took his high-energy pooch with him. The result was a less fit and much plumper me. It is my experience, however, that despite being excellent for you, walking is not enough. We have many more muscles that need to be moved apart from those used in walking.

Since we are no longer chasing animals for food or even walking to the supermarket to buy it, we need to balance this lack of activity with exercise. It changes our body chemistry. We take in more oxygen, adding fuel to every cell. It is now common knowledge that exercise changes the chemistry of the brain, thus benefitting the mind as well. Research has shown that exercise causes an increase in the blood levels of two substances that enhance our well-being, specifically endorphines, which are endogenous opioids (improve mood), and GABA (gamma-aminobutyric acid), a neurotransmitter that aids in relaxation by calming brain activity and reducing anxiety. Consequences of increased GABA are improved mood and brain function (memory, alertness, problem solving), a stronger immune system, and better sleep.

Bear in mind that there are three kinds of exercise that benefit the body in different ways. Using weights strengthens the *muscles*. Aerobic exercises activate the *cardiorespiratory system*, and yoga-type exercises maintain *flexibility of the whole body*. You can go to a gym or join an exercise or yoga class, or you can exercise at home on your own or with a friend. I personally prefer to join a class since I don't have the discipline to exercise regularly at home and always find something else that needs to be done instead. I sign up for a year and make exercise part of my weekly schedule. Exercising in a group with music provides a good break and an opportunity to be with people. The young instructors are usually good role models and give me motivation to exercise. This works for me.

A piece of advice that I remember reading—something that impressed me because it made sense—is that you are as young as your spine is flexible. To maintain flexibility, you need only do the following three movements a few times every day. In the standing position, bend forward and backward (if you are a beginner, then bend forward only and add the backward bend later after a few days if at all); bend sideways; and twist the trunk to each side. Do the same movements with your head to maintain flexibility of the neck. Carry out these movements as far as your body allows, remembering always to move mindfully to avoid strain (especially with the neck exercises).

If standing is difficult or impossible for you, you can exercise while sitting on a chair or stool. If you have back problems, the sitting position eliminates the lower curvature of the spine and takes the pressure off the lower back. Your arms, trunk, and legs are free to move in numerous ways. You can bend the trunk forward, sideways, and obliquely, and you can twist it to each side. Lift and stretch the arms in different directions, and lift the legs. Add the neck exercises. This gives you an excellent workout. I personally enjoy these sitting exercises immensely.

I have recently discovered something new that is becoming popular where I live, especially among the older generation. It is called *Nordic walking* (or pole walking). It involves the use of special poles that are similar to ski poles. These are held in the hands, which swing in rhythm with the legs as in normal walking. The result is a full-body exercise in which the upper- and lower-body muscles are used simultaneously instead of only the lower muscles. It promotes fitness, and since more muscles are used than in ordinary walking, more calories are burned. Amazingly, this more active form of walking is no more tiring than ordinary walking. In addition, there is a reduction in the load carried by the spine and lower limbs since the poles support part of the body's weight. A five-minute instruction session is enough to teach you how to use the poles.

There is a fine article about Nordic walking written by physician Dr. Donald Silverberg, who is now able to take pain-free walks after years of chronic back, hip, and knee pain. Silverberg was introduced to pole walking at the age of seventy-seven, and he was astonished to find relief from the discomfort that numerous kinds of treatments had not relieved. This startling experience led him to search the medical literature for information about this "strange therapy." He found only one paper by a South Korean doctor who employed this kind of walking for elderly women with chronic back pain.

Silverberg ends his article with a poetic appreciation of being able to walk long distances without pain and enjoy the wonders of nature. Clearly, he has found new joy in life, expressed in his quotation of Wordsworth, "My heart with pleasure fills, and dances with the daffodils."

As a result of the previously mentioned article, many local people of an average age of seventy-seven started to practice pole walking. They reported improved mobility and a decline in the severity of their pain. The distance they were able to walk without stopping increased from an average of four hundred meters to one and a half kilometers!

The reference to Dr. Silverberg's article is provided in the bibliography, and it can also be accessed online at www.esra-magazine.com.

***

An enormous amount of research has been done on the *effect of exercise* on health and well-being, and the conclusions are widely known and accepted. However, I am citing two references that I believe are significant.

First, neurologist Dr. David Perlmutter has studied the subject in depth and reports that "the latest science behind the magic of movement in protecting and preserving brain function is stunning—physical exercise is one of the most potent ways of reversing the decline in memory and brain function in elderly humans." In his informative book *Grain Brain,* which describes the negative effects of wheat and other grains on our bodies, Dr. Perlmutter writes that exercise benefits the brain by controlling inflammation, increasing insulin sensitivity, influencing better blood-sugar control, promoting growth of new brain cells, and boosting levels of BDNF (a brain-derived neurological factor that is involved in the creation of new neurons).

Second, a study that was carried out in Israel and published in 2015 in the *Journal of the American Geriatrics Society* examined nine hundred people aged seventy and older who were functioning normally but needed to be hospitalized for acute problems (such as pneumonia or heart problems). The researchers and doctors who conducted the study wanted to understand the reason behind a worldwide phenomenon, namely that a third of people who stay in hospital for treatment may leave in a state of reduced function. Of the hospitalized patients, 46 percent reported reduced functioning as late as a month after being discharged. Findings show for the first time that one of the main factors leading to functional decline among older hospitalized patients is their *reduced mobility* in addition to other risk factors involved with hospitalization itself—such as sleep medications, unnecessary use of catheters, and reduced calorie intake because of fasting before tests and a lack of appetite. This study confirms the need for remaining mobile while hospitalized (as reported by Judy Siegel in *The Jerusalem Post* on May 1, 2015).

Dancing—An Excellent Form of Exercise for the Elderly

Dancing is an excellent form of aerobic exercise at any age. Obviously, different types of dance are suitable for different age groups, and a low-impact form such as simple ballroom is especially good for improving fitness in older adults.

The first review on the physical benefits of dance for older adults was published by Justin Keogh, Andrew Kilding, Phillipa Pidgeon, Linda Ashley, and Dawn Gillis (2009). The available evidence led these authors to conclude that dancing can improve cardiovascular function, lower-body muscle strength and flexibility, balance, agility, and gait in older adults. This reduces the prevalence of falls and cardiovascular risks. The authors recommend the promotion of dance programs that maximize the gains in physical fitness while ensuring safety and enjoyment. In addition, the benefits of the social interaction that dancing provides are obvious.

In her book *Smart Moves*, Carla Hannaford cites studies illustrating that "elderly people who dance regularly decrease their risk of dementia/Alzheimer's Disease by 76% and those that play an instrument by 69%. Both activities are physical, use cross-lateral movements, are playful and are stimulating to the memory."

In short, dancing promotes both physical and mental well-being. And if you don't know how to dance, don't let that stop you. Nobody cares how you dance. Just move to the music. Music is uplifting, and adding movement makes it all the more fun and beneficial to people of all ages.

Unlike medication, the side effects of exercise are all beneficial and can be summarized as follows:

- improved bodily function;
- increased energy and vitality;
- release of mood-affecting hormones (e.g., endorphins) that reduce depression;
- release of GABA, a neurotransmitter that has a calming effect on the brain;
- improved brain function (memory, alertness, problem solving); and
- improved sleep.

Since dancing 'happens' with music, I would like to share some of the latest information regarding the *healing power of music*, focusing on its benefits for the elderly.

Recent studies have found that music may stimulate memory in people with dementia because it activates neural areas and pathways in several parts of the brain. Music has also been shown to improve sleep in patients with dementia and enhance their emotional well-being. Rhythm is used to help stroke survivors and Parkinson's sufferers regain movement.

An aspect of music that is being used to treat people with neurological impairment is *singing*. When a stroke affects areas of the brain that control speech, it can leave patients with an inability to speak fluently (a condition known as nonfluent aphasia). Therapists have noted over the years that people with nonfluent aphasia can sometimes sing words they cannot otherwise say.

These and other benefits of music are well documented in the article "The Healing Power of Music" by Thompson and Schlaug in *Scientific American MIND* (a special edition of *Scientific American*). These authors describe many studies in which music has been used to treat various types of neurological impairment in both young and elderly persons. The attempts to understand how these therapies work at the neurological level are presented. A possible explanation is that these treatments help to restore function by recruiting undamaged areas of the brain.

Recently, I saw a documentary on television about aging and retirement homes. It showed an immobile elderly woman sitting in her room, totally apathetic to her surroundings. When her volunteer caregiver began gently singing while connecting with her face-to-face, the old woman gradually picked up the melody and visibly came alive! It was an impressive demonstration of the power of music and singing.

Earthing/Grounding

A very simple and natural way to enhance physical well-being that most people have not heard of is to *go barefoot whenever possible.* Centuries ago people went barefoot and slept on the ground. Being in touch with the earth's surface is our natural state, but nowadays most of us never touch the ground at all.

The earth has a natural surface charge that provides healing energy, and our feet have a rich network of nerve endings; however, we insulate them with shoes that have synthetic soles. We also sleep on elevated beds made from insulating materials. We are disconnected from the earth's energies.

The ancient way of living has modern names that we are hearing more often nowadays. It is called earthing or grounding.

> Only recently has the knowledge and significance of this connection been explored and explained by scientific experts in geophysics, biophysics, electrical engineering, electrophysiology, and medicine. We all function electrically on an electric planet. Each of us is a collection of dynamic electrical circuits in which trillions of cells constantly transmit and receive energy in the course of their programmed biochemical reactions. The movement of nutrients and water into the cells is regulated by electric fields, and each type of cell has a frequency range in which it operates. Your heart, brain, nervous system, muscles and immune system are prime examples of electrical subsystems operating within your bioelectrical body.

This explanation is taken from *Earthing—The Most Important Health Discovery Ever!* by Ober et al (2014). It's an important book that examines the subject of earthing in depth and teaches a simple but natural way to enhance physical well-being.

Earthing involves being barefoot outside.

Indoors, earthing is achieved by being in contact with special conductive mats and sheets that are connected to the ground. Ober and his co-authors describe the sense of well-being that many people have reported as a result of earthing, and document scientifically monitored studies that have been carried out on this subject. The conclusion is that the inflation of modern chronic illnesses is due to our having lost connection to our planet's surface electrical energy and the resulting electron deficiency in our bodies (in addition to poor diet, physical inactivity, and other known causes). Reconnecting to the earth's natural surface charges restores the natural electrical state in one's physiology and consistently produces the following benefits:

- rapid reduction of inflammation and chronic pain,
- improved blood circulation,
- improved sleep,
- reduced stress,
- reduced blood pressure,
- enhanced muscle function,
- increased energy, and
- accelerated healing from injuries and surgery.

The benefits of grounding, both outdoors and indoors are easy to achieve. When outdoors, besides walking barefoot, you can ground yourself by sitting on the ground or on a chair with your feet on the ground. Actually, when any part of your body makes contact with the ground, you receive energy from below. Swimming or wading in the ocean is also a great way to ground oneself since saltwater is highly conductive, much more than freshwater. Indoor grounding is done with the aid of grounding pads, bed mats, sheets, and ECG (electrocardiogram) patches. These items act as conductors of the earth's natural energy to the body, and replicate standing barefoot or lying directly on the earth.

The work of Ober et al (ibid.) is a great contribution to our understanding of the bioelectric nature of our physiology. Based on numerous case studies and research, it provides evidence of the beneficial effects of grounding on the body. It also provides guidance on indoor grounding methods. The book presents a paper written by Gaetan Chevalier titled "The Physics of Earthing—Simplified." Chevalier spent twenty years doing research on electrophysiology and biofeedback and another ten on earthing, and he concludes that the contemporary biochemical model of the human body is severely lacking a fundamental understanding of the bioelectrical nature of our physiology. He writes,

> The body is a highly intelligent electrobiochemical system that is strongly influenced by its internal electrical environment. Countless electrical charges within this system regulate countless biochemical reactions, including enzyme activity, protein formation and pH (acid/alkaline) balance." Chevalier explains the science behind the electric charges at the earth's surface and in the atmosphere, as well as in the body, and what happens inside your body when you are grounded. He ends his paper with the following statement: "I find it amazing that at this point in the human time line—the beginning of the twenty-first century—we are just starting to scientifically explore the dynamics and benefits to health that come from direct contact with the electric planet we live on.

"All life on Earth is dependent upon background magnetic energy. In a sense, it is the energy of Mother Earth that cradles living cells in a nurturing and orienting energy environment," writes Richard Gerber, MD, in *Vibrational Medicine.*

Finally, a word of caution to anyone who takes multiple medications and would like to do grounding to improve his health. Since grounding affects various physiological processes in the body, a compounded effect may result with certain medicines. For example, grounding has a blood-thinning effect, reduces inflammation, and enhances thyroid function. Therefore, you would need to monitor your condition and possibly adjust the dosage of your medication.

There is a brief section (appendix) on this subject in the previously mentioned book on earthing, and the authors advise discussing this matter with your doctor.

Chapter 2

Food Allergy/Sensitivity

Very often our health problems are caused by what we eat and drink. The discomfort caused by consuming unsuitable foods, if prolonged, can lead to a serious health disorder.

Skin and nail disorders are easy examples to describe because they are visible and easy to detect. When I was in my teens, I developed a problem with my fingernails. My family doctor gave the condition a name (one that I cannot remember now) and told me there was no treatment for it. I would just have to live with it. Fortunately, I came across some literature that recommended vitamin B complex to improve skin, hair, and nail disorders. I started to take brewer's yeast, and within three weeks I could see an improvement. I have not had this problem since. It was simply a matter of vitamin B deficiency, which I learned about in the excellent books of Adele Davis.

Another personal experience comes from a recent visit to a doctor for joint pain. Both the X-rays and the blood test showed that the pain and swelling in my fingers were due to osteoarthritis (as opposed to rheumatoid arthritis). I asked the doctor whether the problem might be caused by something in my diet. He disregarded my question as being *irrelevant* and prescribed a painkiller for the pain. That was his recommended treatment—period! Subsequently, having become more attuned to what I was putting into my body, I linked my arthritic attacks to certain foods I was eating. It turns out that arthritis can be relieved or even cured with proper diet and lifestyle changes as reported by Lauri M. Aesoph in her book, *How to Eat Away Arthritis*. This author reports numerous case studies where a change in diet greatly reduces the pain and stiffness of both rheumatoid arthritis and osteoarthritis. The book teaches how to test for a food allergy or sensitivity, and identify foods that aggravate the symptoms. Eliminating these foods reverses the arthritic condition and restores health, thus allowing the body to heal itself. Aesoph writes that "wheat is probably the most common arthritis aggravating allergen and definitely near the top of the most allergenic food list." Apart from a true allergy to wheat itself, it is often the gluten component of wheat that is responsible for the symptoms.

My personal experiences with doctors' responses to minor health issues, and the following sections, illustrate how out of touch many doctors are with natural ways of achieving good health. I believe that they do the best they can, considering the stressful conditions inherent in the profession *and* the information provided by the pharmaceutical industry (whose main goal is to make money). They do not have time to be informed about and to involve themselves with the holistic approach, which often takes longer to produce results. It takes longer to find and remove the cause of an ailment and bring the body into balance than to provide a quick fix that may solve the problem at hand but may cause further imbalance that leads to other problems. Many of my friends take four or more prescription drugs every day. No one knows how all these chemicals interact in the body. Changes in mood, energy level, allergies, and organ function are all connected. These are the ways in which the body tells us it is damaged and out of balance, maybe even toxic. Correcting our modern diets and lifestyles and reducing the number of drugs prescribed would be a better way to help the body heal.

Population studies show that arthritis is most common in countries where wheat is the staple food. Cardiologist Arthur Agatston of *The South Beach Diet* fame describes his own experience with morning joint stiffness in his fingers. The stiffness and inflammation were due to osteoarthritis. Avoiding gluten relieved the problem. Dr. Agatston chose to avoid gluten rather than take anti-inflammatory medication, which produces the same results.

Another natural way to alleviate the symptoms of arthritis has become common knowledge among alternative health care providers and some conventional physicians. After years of research and the follow-up of thousands of case studies, it is now accepted that the group of plants commonly called nightshades contain inflammation-inducing alkaloids. The nightshades belong to the plant family Solanacea and include (among others) tomatoes, potatoes, eggplant, and all varieties of peppers. Eliminating these foods from the diet results in a marked improvement in both rheumatoid arthritis and osteoarthritis, or even a full recovery (Dr. Norman Childers), http://www.noarthritis.com/nightshades.htm.

In a highly informative book titled *Prescription for Nutritional Healing,* Phyllis Balch describes the solution to various health problems through correct nutrition. This author came to the field after she and her family suffered from a number of undiagnosed (or misdiagnosed) illnesses. Although expert medical support was available to them, their lives continued to be disrupted by these maladies. Balch was introduced to the relationship between nutrition and well-being by a well-known naturopath and writer named Paavo Airola. This led her to pursue her own intensive research into the science of nutrition, and she was able to transform her own health and that of her family by making radical changes in their diet. They were cured by eliminating the cause of disease rather than treating the symptoms. She shares her knowledge in her book with millions of readers in many different countries.

Disorders caused by food sensitivities and allergies may take a long time to diagnose correctly, mainly because of ignorance regarding the connection between the illness and the dietary cause. More and more people are showing signs of sensitivity or even allergies to gluten, wheat, sugar, milk, and dairy products just to mention the more common ones. Numerous case studies describe chronic digestive-system discomfort or more serious disorders that are difficult to diagnose correctly.

In a *food allergy*, the immune system reacts to a component of the food that is detected as being *foreign* by producing antibodies. The antibodies attach to and neutralize the foreign substance (or antigen), thus protecting the body. The allergy can be confirmed by means of a blood test to detect the presence of relevant antibodies. *When the offending food is removed from the diet, the related health problems are alleviated.* My personal awareness that certain minor health problems occur after a recent binge has alerted me to the substances that caused them. I refer to abdominal discomfort, headaches, or short bouts of depression. By recalling what I consumed the day before or consumed repeatedly over the previous days, I have found that the culprit has been bread or some other wheat-containing food. I first made the connection when I felt ill for a few days after downing a bowl of delicious pasta, specifically fettuccini Alfredo, which was my children's favorite dish in those days. Since then I have avoided pasta (or eat it only in small amounts), but too much bread produces the same effect.

Gluten—Wheat and Other Grains

I want to illustrate the point about allergy and sensitivity to certain foods by focusing on one particular food source previously mentioned, namely *wheat*, which is rich in carbohydrates and also contains the protein gluten. Apart from occurring in wheat, gluten is found in *barley* and *rye*, and it is also a common additive in processed foods, cosmetics, and medicines.

My interest in gluten grew when I came across an interesting book while browsing in a bookshop. The book contained a quiz of ten short questions related to one's health. I quickly did the quiz and found that I had seven of the ten conditions that indicate sensitivity to gluten. The ten conditions listed were: feeling bloated after a meal, diarrhea or constipation, frequent abdominal pain or stomach cramps, frequent headaches, stiff joints on awakening, feeling fatigue after getting adequate sleep, excess mucus/postnasal drip/sinus problems, difficulty keeping mental focus, depression, and frequent skin rashes.

The author of this book, cardiologist Arthur Agatston, states that having even one of these conditions may indicate undiagnosed gluten sensitivity. Needless to say I bought the book, *The South Beach Diet Gluten Solution*, and gained much useful information from it.

About 1 percent of the population in both the United States and Western Europe suffer from an extreme *allergy* to gluten known as *celiac disease*. This is a serious disease in which gluten triggers an immune reaction that leads to a variety of problems (described in the following paragraphs). The immune reaction can be detected by means of a blood test that shows the presence of specific antibodies to the gluten protein. In these people gluten must be avoided completely in order to maintain normal health.

A person may test negative for celiac (negative blood test for the immune reaction) but be *sensitive* to gluten. Gluten sensitivity is more common than celiac disease, but it is less serious. Whereas celiac sufferers are so sensitive to gluten that even a very small amount can make them very sick, gluten sensitivity produces *symptoms similar to celiac* but does not involve an immunological response. It may not require giving up gluten entirely.

Agatston first became aware of the gluten problem through an uncle's medical history. His uncle grew up being underweight even though he ate well, and in his thirties he developed type-1 diabetes. At the age of seventy, he suffered from chronic diarrhea. Eventually, he found a doctor who did the appropriate tests and discovered he had celiac disease. This was the cause of his lifelong medical problems!

Subsequent to this revelation, Agatston developed an interest in the effect of nutrition on one's health, especially the heart (since he was a cardiologist). The responses of his patients to different foods led him to devise the famous South Beach diet, which was written up in a book of the same name. In his follow-up book, *The South Beach Diet Gluten Solution,* he reports numerous case histories of people who were ill for years and were cured only when they were finally diagnosed as celiac sufferers or gluten-sensitive. He gives an in-depth explanation of how gluten affects certain people. In this book Agatston teaches his readers to become gluten aware rather than gluten-phobic since gluten can make some people very sick but not everyone.

In celiac sufferers, ingested gluten causes damage to the small intestine. The lining of the small intestine comprises microscopic hairlike outgrowths called villi. These increase the absorptive surface area of the lining and contain specialized cells that enhance absorption of the nutrients from the food we eat. In the case of celiac sufferers, the gluten protein causes extensive damage to the villi, thus greatly reducing the efficiency of the small intestine to absorb the nutrients from food. Physical damage to the villi can be confirmed by taking a biopsy of the wall of the small intestine. In addition, gluten triggers an inflammatory response and, as mentioned earlier, an immune reaction, which is detected by the presence of antibodies to the gluten protein (Agatston).

The symptoms of celiac disease vary from person to person, and they can range from very mild to severe. They include disorders of the digestive system such as stomach pains, bloating, diarrhea or constipation, nausea and vomiting, flatulation, headaches, joint pain, liver abnormalities, ulcers in the mouth, tiredness, hair loss, and depression. Not everyone who suffers from celiac disease exhibits all of these symptoms, but because some of them are easily mistaken for other disorders such as irritable bowel syndrome, it can take a long time before an accurate diagnosis is made. Undiagnosed celiac disease can cause much damage since repeated exposure to gluten affects numerous bodily systems. The most commonly reported problems, however, relate to the digestive tract.

In celiac disease the whole body, including the brain, is affected by inflammation (Perlmutter).

Regarding *gluten sensitivity* (as opposed to allergy), a person may be gluten-sensitive and go undiagnosed for years because "many doctors—even gastroenterologists—are still unaware of the full spectrum of gluten-related disorders, and gluten sensitivity is only now being recognized as a distinct condition. Many symptoms of gluten sensitivity such as headaches and chronic fatigue are dismissed by physicians as 'psychological' but they are very much physical and treatable" (Agatston).

Since there are no medical tests for gluten sensitivity, the best way to determine if a person is sensitive is to remove gluten from the diet completely for a month and observe whether his health has improved. If the symptoms return after gluten is reintroduced into the diet, then it is clear that this person is sensitive to gluten.

Since gluten occurs in grains such as wheat, rye, and barley, it is present in all breads and products made from these grains. The gluten is a required ingredient that gives elasticity to the dough, helping it to rise and keep its shape. Concentrated gluten is often added to bread dough to increase its elasticity and improve the texture of the bread. It is added as a thickener in sauces, marinades, salad dressings, and canned and prepackaged soups.

In recent times there has been an increase in both the consumption of wheat products (usually in the form of highly refined flour) and of gluten, which is added to commercially processed foods. Numerous medical reports have made it obvious that this *increase in wheat consumption* coincides with the time frame during which celiac disease has increased (as have the epidemics of obesity and diabetes).

Scientists believe that the problems presented by wheat consumption are due to one or both of the following reasons:

(1) The wheat our ancestors ate was a perfectly wholesome food, but around 1900, millers discovered that refined flour would keep longer than whole wheat flour. Refining removes the germ of the wheat and all its fiber and leaches out almost all vitamins and minerals. Refined foods and a lack of fiber cause diverticulosis, a common ailment among adult Americans (Lauri Aesoph).

(2) The genetic changes introduced into agricultural crops over the past fifty years resulted in wheat that is genetically different from the ancestral strains. "The products made from modern wheat contain forms of protein never before encountered by humans" (cardiologist William Davis, author of *Wheat Belly*).

Davis provides information on the changes that modern wheat has undergone over the last fifty years because of agricultural practices. Genetic changes have been induced by the crossbreeding of different strains to increase the *yield per acre* and decrease production costs. The result is that the breads, biscuits, and pancakes of today are different from those our grandmothers made. "They might look the same, even taste much the same, but there are biochemical differences. Small changes in wheat protein structure can spell the difference between a devastating immune response to wheat protein versus no immune response at all." While the genetic changes were being introduced, no questions were asked about whether the new strains were compatible with human health. It was simply assumed that the new strains would be perfectly well tolerated by the consuming public. Research findings of agricultural geneticists show that approximately 95 percent of the proteins in the new hybrid strains are the same as in the two parents, while 5 percent are unique and found in neither parent. Fourteen new gluten proteins that were not present in the parent plants have been reported in the offspring of genetic crosses. Apart from the biochemistry, modern wheat crops look different from the ancestral wild species. They have been modified to grow shorter, and in the field all the plants are of uniform height, which facilitates harvesting. (References to relevant scientific publications are given throughout Davis's book).

Davis's research shows that apart from celiac disease and intestinal inflammation (unrelated to celiac disease), there is a direct connection between wheat consumption and diabetes (both type 1 and type 2), weight, skin rashes, body pH, acid-base balance, and aging. He has gathered all the data, and he does what virtually nobody else has done. He dares to question conventional advice that advocates unrestrained consumption of the new modern strains of wheat. Dr. Davis reveals an interesting fact. Consumption of whole wheat and other whole grains raises blood glucose levels more that sugar does!

When he helps his overweight, diabetes-prone patients on ways to reduce blood sugar, he advises the elimination of wheat and wheat-based foods from the diet. After three months, blood tests show that in most patients, the blood glucose drops from the diabetic range to normal. *Diabetics become nondiabetics by removal of carbohydrates, especially wheat, from the diet.* Many of the patients also lose most of their extra weight. But what astounded Davis most at first was that his patients reported that symptoms of acid reflux disappeared and the cyclic cramping and diarrhea or irritable bowel syndrome were gone. Their energy levels improved. They had greater focus and slept better. Rashes disappeared, even rashes that had been present for many years. Rheumatoid arthritis pain improved or disappeared, enabling patients to cut back or even eliminate the medications used to treat it. Asthma symptoms improved or resolved completely, allowing many to throw away their inhalers.

According to Davis, there are hundreds of conditions that have been associated with celiac disease and/or immune-mediated gluten intolerance. The consequences of gluten consumption are mind-boggling. "Thinking of celiac disease as just diarrhea, as is often the case in many doctors' offices, is an enormous, and potentially fatal, oversimplification."

Gluten is found in other grains besides wheat, namely rye, barley, spelt, triticale, kamut, and bulgur. Oats do not contain gluten but must be avoided by celiac sufferers because oats are often processed in the same equipment as wheat and consequently may contain traces of wheat.

Gluten-free grains, such as millet (sorghum), quinoa, amaranth, and teff, can be safely consumed by individuals who are allergic or intolerant to gluten or wheat. Buckwheat (also known as kasha) is not a grain and does not contain gluten.

A disorder that differs from celiac disease and gluten-sensitivity is *wheat allergy* as described by both Davis and Agatston. It causes an immune response to a component of wheat, but the condition differs from celiac disease in that the allergic reaction occurs within minutes to hours after exposure. In severe cases an acute asthma-like reaction may occur, causing difficulty in breathing. Allergic or anaphylactic reactions (severe reactions resulting in shock) are caused by nongluten proteins found in wheat. Exposure in susceptible individuals triggers nasal congestion, hives, rashes (atopic dermatitis and urticaria), and a curious and dangerous condition called wheat-dependent exercise-induced anaphylaxis (WDEIA), in which rash, asthma, or anaphylaxis are provoked during exercise. WDEIA is most commonly associated with wheat but can also occur with shellfish. Such anaphylactic reactions can be relieved by administering the antidote epinephrine by injection (Agatston).

Agatston warns us to be vigilant about exposure to wheat. "Wheat and gluten come in a dizzying variety of forms. Cous-cous, matzo, orzo, graham, and bran are all wheat. So are faro, panko, and rusk. Appearances can be misleading. For instance, the majority of breakfast cereals contain wheat flour, wheat-derived ingredients, or gluten, despite names such as Corn Flakes or Rice Crispies."

Neurologist David Perlmutter deals with the adverse effects of wheat and gluten on the *brain* in his book *Grain Brain.* Perlmutter is also an expert on nutrition and a founding member of the American Board of Integrative and Holistic Medicine. He gives convincing evidence of the harmful effects of carbohydrates on the brain and expounds on the necessity of including fat in our diets. He believes that gluten is a modern poison and blames it for numerous ailments, including digestive disturbances (bloating, diarrhea, constipation, cramping, gas), diabetes, sugar cravings, hives/rashes, malabsorption of food, migraines, arthritis, nausea, brain fog, depression, seizures/epilepsy, neurological disorders (dementia, Alzheimer's, schizophrenia), among others.

Perlmutter states that "we have known for more than thirty years that wheat increases blood sugar more than table sugar, but we still somehow think that this is not possible. It seems counterintuitive. But it's a fact that few foods produce as much of a surge in blood glucose as those made with wheat." He also reports that whole-wheat bread is on a par with white bread as far as conversion to sugar is concerned. Perlmutter's statements support Davis's theory that eliminating wheat is a fast track way to lower blood sugar levels, reduce weight, and reverse the progression of diabetes.

Carbohydrates and Sugar

We are exposed to high amounts of *sugar* on a daily basis. Not only is it present in wheat and other starch-rich foods from which it is derived, but it is *added* to most processed foods. Sugar is found (in its different forms) in unexpected places such as salad dressings, ketchup, barbeque sauce, bread buns, and virtually all commercially prepared, prepacked foods. Beverages are known to be loaded with sugar, and sugar is added to low-fat processed foods to improve the taste. The consumption of sugar increased more than 30 percent in the last three decades, representing the most drastic change to which the human body has ever been subjected! This is believed to be a major contributor to the increasing incidence of obesity and chronic metabolic diseases.

The medical profession is becoming more aware of the relationship between sugar and diseases such as diabetes, high blood pressure, heart disease, and dementia. A pediatrician named Dr. Robert Lustig, who treats childhood obesity, claims that sugar (in excess) is a poison, and that obesity is symptomatic of an addiction to sugar.

He has witnessed a rapid increase in the occurrence of obesity, fatty liver disease, and type-2 diabetes in young children. He is seeing heart disease in teenagers! Lustig is especially vocal and active in trying to change the way children are lured to sugar-laden foods and beverages through clever advertising. He is waging a war against the increased use of sugar in processed foods, and believes that the food industry should not be given carte blanche. "They are allowed to make money, but they are not allowed to make money by making people sick." Lustig presents his research and arguments in his book *Fat Chance: Beating the Odds Against Sugar, Processed Food, Obesity and Disease.*

Diabetes is a serious condition because a person may be diabetic and not know it. It cannot be detected through clearly identifiable symptoms, and by the time a person seeks medical advice, complications may already have set it. These complications can lead to blindness, kidney failure, and lower limb amputation. For all of these reasons, diabetes has been called the "silent killer."

Sugar is *hidden* in many of the food labels on the products we buy. It is included under names such as carbohydrates, glucose, dextrose, fructose, corn syrup, malt syrup, barley malt, rice syrup, caramel, molasses, cane juice crystals, honey, among others. (Honey contains a variety of sugars as well as proteins and minerals.)

Most fat-free (and gluten-free) foods are packed with carbohydrates. One of the problems associated with low-fat or no-fat processed foods is that they need additives to improve the taste and are spiked with sugars (among other substances) to solve this problem. The American Heart Association recommends a daily intake of six to nine teaspoons of sugar a day. However, we unwittingly consume much more than this—seventeen teaspoons of added sugar per day in Britain, twenty teaspoons per day in the United States (Lustig).

A brief explanation of the term _carbohydrates_ seems appropriate here for anyone who does not know the full meaning. _Carbohydrates_ are the chemical form in which plants and animals (including humans) store energy. They include _starch_ (present in high amounts in plant foods such as white rice, potatoes, peas, beans, and grains), _glycogen_ (present in red meat and liver), and _cellulose_ (which constitutes the nondigestible fiber parts of our vegetable diet).

Starch, glycogen, and cellulose are all long-chained polymers composed entirely of _glucose_. These polymers differ in the types of chemical bonds that bind the glucose molecules together, resulting in chains that may be straight or branched. They are referred to as "complex carbohydrates."

In the body, starch and glycogen are broken down into their constituent _glucose_ molecules, which are then used directly by the cells for the _production of energy_ or other purposes as needed. If glucose is present in excessive amounts, it may be converted into fat. _Blood tests for "sugar" measure the concentration of glucose in the blood._ Glucose, a six-carbon molecule, is the most abundant monosaccharide (single sugar) in nature. It also goes by the name _dextrose_.

Fruit sugar or _fructose_ is also a monosaccharide, but it contains five carbons. Fructose is metabolized by the liver. Excess amounts are converted to fat, which is then dispatched to our fat cells. Table sugar or _sucrose_ is a disaccharide made up of one molecule each of glucose and fructose. Milk sugar or _lactose_ is also a disaccharide composed of glucose and galactose. All these names end with the suffix "ose," which denotes a sugar. _Sugars_ are included under the general term _carbohydrate_.

I have added this information to enable readers who do not have a background in biology or chemistry to more easily understand the ingredients listed on the labels of food products in the stores. For a more in-depth discussion of the chemistry of carbohydrates, I recommend the book *Lehninger Principles of Biochemistry* by Nelson and Cox.

Wheat and other grains are rich in carbohydrates in the form of starch. Knowing that starch (from whatever source) is composed entirely of glucose molecules helps us to understand why wheat and other starch-rich foods must be avoided by people suffering from diabetes. As mentioned previously, eating bread results in higher blood glucose than consuming table sugar. The reason is that upon digestion, starch breaks down entirely to glucose while sugar (sucrose) consists of glucose and fructose in equal parts. Glucose affects insulin production while the fructose is metabolized in the liver.

I know someone who is diabetic but eats bread, pasta, and potato gnocchi in abundant quantities, and if you can believe it, he is in the medical profession! Clearly, he is ignorant of the relationship between starch and blood sugar.

Sugar in itself is not a toxin. Sucrose (table sugar) is extracted from harmless plants that we grow as crops (sugar cane in tropical and warm temperate areas, and sugar-beet in cooler and temperate climates). No one suggests that carbohydrates and sugar must be completely omitted from our diets as they are needed for the production of energy. The problem with our modern diet is that they are ubiquitous, and we unwittingly consume them in excess. The end result is that the body becomes overloaded with sugar, and this causes the pancreas to produce more insulin. The higher the blood sugar, the more insulin must be pumped from the pancreas and made available to the cells. As the insulin increases, cells become less and less responsive to the insulin signal (and do not metabolize the sugar). As the situation progresses, the pancreas finally maximizes its output of insulin, but it is still not enough. At this point the cells lose their ability to respond and ultimately blood sugar levels rise, resulting in type-2 diabetes (Perlmutter). The excess sugar is converted to fat in the liver, leading to fatty liver and heart disease.

British scientist and nutritionist John Yudkin studied the available data on heart disease. He found a correlation between increased heart disease and increased consumption of sugar, *not fat*. As early as the 1970s, his laboratory experiments on animals and humans showed, as other experiments had done before, that excess sugar is processed into fat in the liver before entering the bloodstream. His hypothesis that sugar and not fat contributes to heart disease *posed a threat to the sugar industry*. He faced vicious opposition from an industry that offers deceitful advertising, claiming sugar to be an essential component of the human diet. A well-known cereal manufacturer once ran advertisements convincing parents that its sugary breakfast cereals were equivalent in nutritional value to bacon and eggs! Mimicking the history of tobacco, the sugar industry funds research to the tune of millions of dollars and thus determines which questions should be asked and which answers are the most suitable (to its interests).

Epidemiologic studies carried out about forty years ago suggested that the risk of heart disease increases with high *fat* intake. This was associated with high cholesterol levels. People were advised to reduce their fat consumption, and grain-based foods began to fill the calorie gap. Cardiologist William Davis says that the advice of reducing fats in the diet and increasing the consumption of grains is *faulty*, a fiction story that benefits the processed-food industry. "It triggered an explosion of processed food products, most requiring just a few pennies worth of basic materials. Wheat flour, cornstarch, high-fructose corn syrup, sucrose, and food coloring are now the main ingredients of products that fill the interior aisles of any modern supermarket. Revenues for Big Food companies swelled."

It has become clear to researchers that when we drastically reduce the intake of fats and eat excessive carbohydrates, our body sends out an alarm that triggers the liver to produce a large amount of cholesterol. "The only way to stop this internal pathway from running amok is to consume an adequate amount of dietary cholesterol and back way off on carbs," writes Perlmutter.

I have focused on gluten, wheat, and carbohydrates because of my own personal experience with "wheat overload." I like bread and also indulge in other high-carbohydrate foods. Apparently, I don't feel bad enough to be forced to stop, but I can say with certainty that too much of these foods adversely affect my health. Recently, for almost a year, I had headaches every single day. Taking a painkiller in order to be able to sleep became part of my nightly routine. At the time I was eating about four slices of bread every day. Then I reduced this to one slice per day, and my headaches stopped! Other symptoms that I can link to wheat overload are bloating, abdominal sensitivity, and the occasional bout of depression.

Many years ago I knew someone who was on a strict wheat-free diet—a concept that was foreign to me then. When I asked her what would happen if she ate something containing wheat, she told me that she would become depressed or even suicidal. I dismissed this as an unlikely story but never forgot it. Today I know that I am definitely sensitive to gluten/wheat. It seems that my body can tolerate a small amount, but over a certain threshold, the symptoms begin to appear.

Contrary to conventional knowledge, which has been telling us that *fat* causes atherosclerosis (blockage of the arteries), Davis describes how _carbohydrates_ cause *atherosclerotic plaque* to accumulate in our arteries! Atherosclerotic plaque is a major cause of heart attacks. He is supported by neurologist David Perlmutter, whose work refutes the advice we have been given about avoiding fat and triglycerides based on a new understanding and new ways of interpreting blood-test data. He tells us that the body needs cholesterol as it plays a role in normal brain function.

I highly recommend the books by Agatston, Davis, and Perlmutter cited previously. They are packed with information about the effect of carbohydrates on our health, and they are based both on research and case studies, as well as on their professional experience. They explain how carbohydrates and fats are metabolized in the body and affect our physiology. *They are telling us that carbohydrates are more harmful than fat and are responsible for the increase in obesity, high blood pressure, heart disease, type-2 diabetes, dementia, and other chronic health problems.*

These authors also provide gluten-free recipes and practical guidance on how to avoid wheat and gluten.

Aside from wheat, gluten, and carbohydrates, much can be said about sensitivity/intolerance to other foods and ingredients we consume, including milk and dairy products, caffeine, sodium, and synthetic substances, such as artificial sweeteners and monosodium glutamate that are added to cereals, baked goods, and beverages. There is a wealth of literature available on the omnipresence of these components in our food. A simple Internet search will reveal a great deal of information for anyone who wishes to learn more about this subject.

We consume other *hidden* substances in our foods. For example, the meat we eat comes from animals that are treated with hormones to accelerate their growth and weight gain. Hormones are administered to enhance milk production. Antibiotics are given to cattle and chickens to suppress disease in the overcrowded conditions in which they are raised. Add to this the stress hormones produced by these animals throughout their lives, especially when they are on their way to being slaughtered. In addition, we consume pesticide residues in fruits and vegetables, chemicals in the water we drink, unsafe cookware, and others. The list is endless.

> Chemicals: Noxious substances from
> which modern foods are made.
>
> —Source unknown

Chapter 3

Toxins Everywhere

I think it is important to write about the nonstick materials that coat the pots and pans we cook our food in. The *nonstick coating* is commonly referred to as Teflon, the original manufacturer's brand name. It is a plastic known to release toxic fluorocarbon gases at very high temperatures. An added concern is the material that binds this plastic layer to the cooking utensil, namely perfluorooctanic acid (PFOA). The latter breaks down at high temperatures, releasing poisons into the food. After prolonged use, the surface layer of nonstick cookware may get scratched/eroded. Utensils that are thus damaged should be discarded. The American Environmental Protection Agency (EPA) reports that the chemicals in Teflon coatings are potentially carcinogenic and that the high levels found in human blood samples are associated with a greater risk of thyroid disease, heart disease, and stroke. It is estimated that 98 percent of the US population has detectable levels of PFOA in their blood.

High levels of exposure to the gases released from nonstick cookware produce flu-like symptoms referred to as "Teflon flu" or "polymer fume fever." Commonly reported symptoms are headaches, coughing, chills, and fever, which develop several hours after inhalation of the gases. (Laboratory tests have shown that these gases are lethal to birds.) Manufacturers refuse to admit that their cookware is harmful to human health. But thankfully, the manufacturing process has been revised, and PFOA is currently being phased out. Some of the nonstick cookware on sale now carries the label "PFOA-free." An important piece of advice from some manufacturers is that empty cookware should not be left on a hot stove or in a hot oven. This advice may sound superfluous, but preheating may be common practice. (My son used to routinely preheat Teflon cookware before adding the food, sometimes leaving it empty on the heat for long periods.) The higher-quality brands now carry instructions to use the utensils at low to medium heat, or warnings not to exceed a maximum temperature of 260 degrees Celsius.

Further information regarding the health risks of nonstick cookware can be obtained from articles on the Internet.

Another chemical of concern that we are exposed to daily is *Bisphenol A* (BPA), a component of polycarbonate—the hard, clear plastic that goes into water bottles, baby bottles, food containers, medical devices, and dental sealants. It is also used in the lining of food and beverage cans. Chemically, BPA is an estrogen-mimicking compound and therefore may be disruptive to the endocrine system. The chemical can leach out of plastics and the lining of cans and into the food. In animal experiments it has been shown that at high concentrations it adversely affects the reproductive system. There has been controversy regarding the effect of BPA on humans, and in 2010, the US Food and Drug Administration (FDA) finally began to express concern about the potentially harmful effects on children. Now many manufacturers of baby bottles and food formula cans have stopped using BPA in their products (see www.webmed.com and http://articles.mercola.com). Studies show that almost everyone has traces of this chemical in the body, and the major exposure route is believed to be our diet.

In 2015, a survey carried out in the United States of 250 brands of canned food found that more than 40 percent still use BPA-lined cans. "The biggest problem is people have no reliable way of knowing whether they are buying food that is laced with this toxic chemical" —because Federal regulations do not require canned goods to disclose BPA-based linings.

http://www.scientificamerican.com/article/bpa-still-widely-used-in-canned-goods.

Another source of harmful substances that I long suspected but only recently paid attention to, is the convenient *tea bag* that most of us use daily. I quote a section from an article by Dr. Joseph Mercola, a nutrition expert who writes extensively on health issues: "Paper tea bags are frequently treated with epichlorohydrin, which hydrolyzes to 3-MCPD when coming into contact with water. 3-MCPD is a carcinogen associated with food processing that has also been implicated in infertility and suppressed immune function" (http://articles.mercola.com).

A Canadian government scientific report confirms that epichlorohydrin is used in the manufacture of tea bags and other products. "Epichlorohydrin was identified as a potential concern to human health based on its classification by an international organization, as a substance which was found to cause cancer in some studies with laboratory animals." The government of Canada has determined that epichlorohydrin is considered to be harmful to human health and is proposing that this chemical be added to the cosmetic ingredient hotlist to prevent its future use in cosmetics.

"Polymers made from epichlorohydrin are used in *paper reinforcement* and in the food industry to manufacture tea bags, coffee filters, and sausage/salami casings as well as in water purification. This chemical is added to pulp during the paper-making process *to promote the wet-strength of the paper*" (italics added). There are other references that can be found on the Internet related to the use of this chemical.

Despite the facts mentioned above, Canadians are told they do not need to take any specific actions to reduce their exposure since "exposure to epichlorohydrin is very low."

Some tea bags are made with plastic, such as nylon, thermoplastic, PVC or polypropylene. While these plastics have high melting points, the temperature at which the molecules in polymers begin to break down is always lower than the melting point, which could allow the bags to leach compounds of unknown health hazards into your tea when steeped in boiling water (http://articles.mercola.com/sites/articles/archive/2013/04/24/tea-bags.aspx).

So there is evidence that tea bags contain potentially harmful substances. Since "the dose makes the poison," it is advisable to keep a watch on how you feel after you have had numerous cups of tea in a single day. I am not aware of any research that has looked at the direct effect of this on our health. You may think that if all this is true, then we should all be sick. Well, unfortunately, many of us have a health complaint most of the time or experience health disturbances that appear out of the blue. I believe we should be concerned about the previously mentioned risk only if we use a very large number of tea bags every day. I personally try to limit my intake of tea made with tea bags to two or three a day, but often I have more. I have not completely changed my tea-drinking habits, but I think that the best option is to use loose tea leaves. This may seem less convenient, but brewing tea this way soon becomes part of the routine as it was in the "old days" not so long ago.

Unfortunately, whether it comes in bags or as loose leaves, tea has been found to contain high levels of pesticides. Vast areas of tea cultivation are vulnerable to agricultural pests, and farmers are obligated to protect their crops against diseases. Pesticide use in tea continues to be a hotly contested issue. An article written in June

2015 that lists the toxic chemicals used in tea plantations (and found in our brewed tea) states,

> A Canadian Food Inspection Agency study that was published in the Journal of Agricultural and Food Chemistry in 2014 found that many pesticides not only made it into people's cupboards but also into the tea itself. Demand for tea is still massive around the world, but the countries that have the largest plantations may not have the regulations in place to forbid or limit the use of certain pesticides, such as DDT, that are banned in other parts of the world. (https://www.chemservice.com/news/2015/06/which-pesticides-are-in-your-tea-cup)

There is a certain brand of tea that gives me a headache if I have more than one cup a day. I always wondered why. It happens to be listed in the previously mentioned article as containing high levels of pesticides.

While on the subject of tea (and other hot beverages), watch out for the *disposable Styrofoam and paper cups* that are freely available at coffee machines. Styrofoam is a (polystyrene) plastic, and paper cups are often lined with plastic or wax to prevent liquid from soaking through the paper or leaking out. Research carried out in 1988 reported the presence of styrene in human fatty tissue (reported in an article in http://www.healthbeckon.com/drink-coffee-styrofoam-cups-research-says-hazardous).

The styrene monomer in the plastic is a neurotoxin and suspected carcinogen, and it causes a host of other adverse health effects such as the following:

- irritation and mucous secretion from eyes and nose,
- increased levels of fatigue and decreased ability to concentrate,

- increased levels of abnormal pulmonary function and cancer, and
- disruption of hormonal function resulting in thyroid and other hormone related problems.

Needless to say, plastic containers should never be used in the microwave oven to heat or cook food (http://www.dailymail.co.uk/health/article-2709577/Do-foam-cups-contain-cancer-causing-chemicals-Leading-panel-says-styrene-human-carcinogen.html).

One wonders why food and beverages are still allowed to be sold in plastic containers. The answer is that "further research is needed" to prove that all the evidence is meaningful before the chemicals are regulated by the authorities.

Apart from the health risks posed by ingested poisonous residues, the *environmental impact* of the mass production of plastics and paper is obvious. The manufacturing processes use enormous amounts of water and toxic chemicals, while the plastic end products take hundreds of years to decompose.

Pesticides

Most of us have a horror of pesticides, and rightly so. Many of them are poisonous chemicals that are harmful or even deadly to humans, animals, and the environment. *However*, there are laws and regulations in place that protect us from exposure to high levels of these chemicals, which are used in large quantities in agriculture against plant pests.

The World Health Organization (WHO) and the government departments of health and the environment in Europe and the United States, have examined thousands of studies and trials on this subject. They have devised regulations that manufacturers and farmers are obligated to adopt to ensure the safe handling and controlled use of pesticides. In addition, they have fixed the maximum residue levels (MRLs) that are allowed on fruits and vegetables. MRLs are defined as the highest level of a pesticide residue that is legally tolerated on/in food and animal feed. In most countries these levels are enforceable by law, and they cover locally grown as well as imported foods. They are just one of the safeguards in place to reduce exposure to pesticides. The old adage "The dose makes the poison" holds here too.

Plants are vulnerable to airborne and soilborne pathogens, attack by insects, and competition for water and space by fast-growing weeds. These pests can devastate entire plantations of food crops. Without the use of pesticides (commonly referred to as plant protection products), farmers would not be able to deliver enough food to the billions of mouths on the planet. This was brought home to me very clearly when I witnessed the results of field trials in which the controls (the plants growing without pesticides) were damaged or totally destroyed.

The *responsible use* of these chemicals according to the regulations is essential to minimize our exposure to this "necessary evil."

***

We are indeed exposed to numerous potentially harmful substances every day, both in the environment and in our modern diet, not to mention the utensils we use. Is it any wonder that most of us feel under the weather much of the time? The best we can do is to minimize our contact with such substances.

On the brighter side, we should remember that our bodies have the capacity to overcome the adverse effects of exposure to small amounts of harmful substances. The body is endowed with an *intelligence* that strives toward balance and good health. When we give it too much of anything—whether natural food ingredients or added chemicals—we upset the balance. "The dose makes the poison" is an adage that indicates a basic principle of toxicology, namely that excessive amounts of anything, even relatively harmless stuff, can overtax the body and lead to illness. I have learned this through my own experience with something as simple (and beneficial) as fruit! For a long period during my youth, I used to eat an orange every morning. At a certain stage, I reckoned that having more oranges every day would be even better for me, right? Wrong! Eating three oranges in one day upsets my digestive system and causes diarrhea. The same is true with coffee. When I am very tired and drink a lot of coffee to perk me up, I end up feeling worse. Four cups of coffee a day for two or more consecutive days gives me severe headaches and makes me feel drained of energy. The same happens with bread, which I find difficult to resist. As with coffee, there seems to be a cumulative effect, with the bad results showing up after two or so days of indulgence.

The bottom line is that we need to *know* our bodies and how much of what we consume becomes too much. We need constantly to be aware of how we feel, health-wise. Whenever something is out of whack, the origin of the discomfort should be traced so that we will know to avoid the causative substance or at least reduce its presence in our bodies.

***

This section on physical well-being focuses on the areas that are of interest to me personally. There are, of course, many other important issues related to our physical well-being that are worthy of discussion but have not been dealt with here.

Chapter 4

Our Health At the Mercy of Medicine and Industry

We cannot live without modern (conventional) medicine. It saves lives, repairs broken bodies, prevents epidemics, and kills harmful pathogens. However, it often causes harm unintentionally. It is well known that most medications result in harmful side effects. Moreover, there are treatments such as chemotherapy that produce awful effects on the body.

Medicine has evolved into a vast number of specializations as more and more information on every part of our anatomy accumulates. Unfortunately, treatment of one organ in isolation can result in gross imbalance of the rest of the body, and this is something that modern medicine and most doctors often do not take into account. Alternative medicine (defined in chapter 5) takes a holistic approach by considering the state of the whole person. It regards illness as a sign of imbalance and strives to restore balance to the body.

Dealing with health disorders by only treating the symptoms is equivalent to the following scenario: Imagine you are traveling in your car when a red light suddenly begins to flash on the dashboard, indicating a dangerously low oil level. Your solution is to take a hammer and bash the light. The result is great. No more flashing light! However, anyone with minimal knowledge of motor mechanics can predict the end of the story.

This is similar to what happens when we have a headache, abdominal pain, or any other discomfort. We are given chemicals to suppress the warning signs. This kind of solution, when applied over long periods or at high doses, produces undesirable results.

Alternative medicine, on the other hand, aims to remove the cause of the disorder and facilitate inner healing. It takes a *holistic* approach by considering the state of the entire body when dealing with a disorder in any organ or part of the body and uses more natural, less invasive intervention.

Ultimately, it is the body that heals itself, and medicine in whatever form it is applied merely facilitates this healing. The truth is that no single approach has all the answers, and to simply dismiss an approach because we don't understand how it works does not benefit us in any way. It makes sense to merge conventional and alternative medicine rather than to exclude either one. As stated by Dr. Eric Pearl, author of *The Reconnection*, "If the natural approach for some reason doesn't work for us, by all means, (modern) medicine is the next logical route. If our body hasn't been able to heal on its own, this is the point where drugs, surgery, or other extreme measures may be necessary."

Before describing the holistic approach to health that is associated with alternative healing methods, I will digress and present evidence of some negative aspects of conventional medicine to which we are all exposed.

Death by medicine is a concept that is gaining recognition despite the enormous technological advances in the medical profession. This term is the title of a report written by a group of five researchers and medical doctors. They analyzed the published literature and statistical evidence relating to ill health and death resulting from hospitalization and adverse reactions to prescribed drugs. The findings from this meticulous study indicated that conventional, government-approved medicine is "the leading cause of death" in the United States. This report is now available as a book with the same title authored by Gary Null and the original researchers and published in 2011.

The report provides figures for unnecessary hospitalizations, unnecessary X-rays, unnecessary surgery and the exaggerated use of antibiotics. It was reported that almost half of patients with upper respiratory tract infections in the United States receive antibiotics from their doctor when 90 percent of upper respiratory infections are viral and should not be treated with antibiotics. Other similar practices have resulted in bacterial resistance to antibiotics, which is now the cause of many hospital-acquired infections.

The FDA reports that medication errors cause at least one death every day and injure approximately 1.3 million people annually in the United States. Medication mishaps are caused by errors in prescribing, dispensing, directions for use, poor understanding by the patients of the directions for use, and ambiguities in product names and abbreviations.

The problem of "medical errors" is a global issue as illustrated by a five-country survey published in the *Journal of Health Affairs*. The breakdown by country showed the percentages of those suffering injury because of a medical or drug error as 18 percent in Britain, 23 percent in Australia and New Zealand, 25 percent in Canada, and 28 percent in the United States.

Sadly, the situation is not improving, and hospitals continue to be *unsafe*. The reasons given by medical administrators always revolve around the lack of resources (money), understaffing, and an increase in contamination caused by virulent bacteria that have become resistant to antibiotics. Scientist and author Bruce Lipton (2005) believes that the massive quantities of drugs prescribed in the United States violate the Hippocratic oath taken by all doctors to *first do no harm*. "We have been programmed by pharmaceutical corporations to become a nation of prescription drug-popping junkies with tragic results." Unfortunately, this sad state of affairs has spilled over into other parts of the world as pharmaceutical companies become globalized. Lipton, author of *The Biology of Belief*, expresses his dismay at the statistics, "especially for a healing profession that has arrogantly dismissed three thousand years of effective Eastern medicine as unscientific, even though it is based on a deeper understanding of the Universe."

According to the statistics published in 2013 by the Center for Disease Control and Prevention (CDC) in the United States, prescription drugs were responsible for more than 482,600 deaths per year. (Illegal drugs such as heroin and cocaine killed 13,201 people, while the number of deaths attributed to marijuana in the same period was zero.) More recently, the American Medical Association reported that pharmaceutical drug side effects are a leading cause of iatrogenic illness (illness because of medical treatment), the latter being the third leading cause of death in the United States.

Most of the cases of drug side effects are not documented as such. It was found that one of the reasons for this failure is that in nearly two-thirds of the cases, doctors could not diagnose drug side effects or failed to heed the warning signs.

Medical doctors are caught in a difficult situation. Besides being pawns in the huge medical industrial complex, their heavy patient loads do not allow them much time to ask all the necessary questions, to keep abreast of each patient's condition, and to identify drug-related symptoms. A serious illness is like a giant jigsaw puzzle with most of the pieces missing. Finding and fitting the missing pieces takes time and in many cases requires expertise in order to get the correct picture. Rather than blaming the doctors, we should be aware that it's the system that has gone awry.

Lipton points out that after graduation, doctors receive their continuing education about pharmaceutical products from representatives of the drug manufacturers in the health-care industry. The industry provides doctors with information about the efficacy of new drugs, but the primary goal is to sell product. Drug companies freely offer this "education" so they can persuade doctors to push their products.

"Pharmaceutical companies identify deviations in physiology and behavior from some *hypothetical norm* as unique disorders. Their advertisements convince the public that they are afflicted with particular maladies that can be cured by their specialized products" (Lipton).

Pills mean money, and so now we have "a pill for every ill."

A good example is the case of *cholesterol*. The upper limit for a healthy blood cholesterol reading used to be 240mg/dl. Then about thirty years ago, we were told that this value is way too high, and our cholesterol levels should be lower than two hundred. This meant that more people had to take cholesterol-lowering drugs. Today the threshold is down to 180. Needless to say, this provides good business for Big Pharma. Fortunately, members of the medical profession are speaking up and objecting to the new threshold values. Neurologist and nutritionist Dr. David Perlmutter in his recent book *Grain Brain* says that taking cholesterol-lowering medication if your blood level is 240 mg/dl is "wrong in thought and action as cholesterol is one of the most critical chemicals in human physiology, especially as it relates to brain health. The brain holds only 2 percent of the body's mass but contains 25 percent of the total cholesterol. One-fifth of the brain by weight is cholesterol." In the brain, cholesterol serves as a powerful antioxidant. Further, it is the precursor of steroid hormones (estrogen and testosterone) as well as vitamin D.

Perlmutter claims that we live in a society that continues to demonize fats and cholesterol in particular, and that the pharmaceutical industry preys on misinformation. It perpetrates falsehoods, many of which could physically destroy us. To support his claims, Perlmutter presents studies from scientific and medical literature involving thousands of patients. "There hasn't been a published study in the last thirty years that has unequivocally demonstrated that lowering serum cholesterol by eating a low-fat, low-cholesterol diet prevents or reduces heart attack or death rate. Eating high-cholesterol foods has no impact on our actual cholesterol levels, and the alleged correlation between higher cholesterol and higher cardiac risk is an absolute fallacy."

More that 80 percent of the cholesterol that is measured in your blood is produced in your own liver. Our bodies make up to two thousand milligrams of cholesterol a day because we need it. The effects of cholesterol-rich foods (including eggs) on blood cholesterol are small and clinically insignificant. The belief that the cholesterol we eat converts directly into blood cholesterol is false. Perlmutter believes that we need to consume an adequate amount of dietary cholesterol and back off carbohydrates. The high-cholesterol patients who go on his diet can safely reduce their levels to normal without drugs while enjoying cholesterol-rich foods.

Just recently, the US government announced its intention to *withdraw* a long-standing warning about cholesterol. It follows a change in the thinking of many nutritionists who now believe that cholesterol intake for a healthy adult may not significantly affect blood cholesterol levels or increase the risk of heart disease.

Another example of changing (hypothetical) norms is found in the guidelines for the prevention and management of *high blood pressure*. For many years doctors considered a systolic/diastolic reading of 120/80 to be ideal, and any value below 140/90 to be fine. Then in 2003, the US Department of Health and the National Institutes of Health (NIH) declared that systolic pressure of 120 could be unsafe! They established a new condition called *prehypertension* for systolic pressure of 120–139, recommending treatment with hypertension drugs. In 2014, new guidelines were published (*JAMA* 311[5]: 538), setting the threshold at 140/90 for people under sixty years of age. For people older than sixty, 150/90 is the new threshold, implying that those whose systolic pressure is less than 150 are taking blood pressure medications unnecessarily.

***

Different researchers focus on different aspects of human health and diet. I suppose it partly depends on the personal interest of each scientist, but more probably, it depends on the funding that is available to the research laboratory where he works. In the past, governments used to provide most of the funding to universities and research institutions. However, in most countries budget cuts resulted in much of this support drying up, and industry became the major source of funding. This has led to the vested interests of industrial companies influencing the type of research being done, and even the results that are accepted for publishing. Industry has the power and the money to promote its opinion; researchers do not.

A simple Internet search reveals numerous formal and informal writings about the influence of the pharmaceutical industry on medical practices. One such entry refers to John Abraham, who wrote *Overdosed America*. He says that many of the articles published in respected medical journals seem like infomercials whose purpose is to promote their sponsors' products rather than to search for the best way to improve people's health. His research revealed a scandal in which medical studies were rigged. Research findings that didn't come out in the sponsor's favor were omitted. According to Abraham, a lid on this kind of corruption is sealed by a complex web of corporate influence that includes disempowered regulatory agencies, commercially sponsored medical education, brilliant advertising, expensive public-relations campaigns, and manipulation of free media coverage. As a result, the drug and medical devices industries are raking in unheard-of profits, while the health-care costs for people have increased enormously.

When industry is confronted by complaints about the harmful effects of its products, we are told that "more research is needed" to prove that the complaints are justified. It is common knowledge that in the past, tobacco companies hid the dangers of smoking while they continued to advertise their cigarette brands. There used to be TV advertisements showing medical doctors in their white coats as they were smoking, thus implying that smoking was beneficial to health. One particular brand boasted that "more doctors smoke Camels." The concern about the harm caused by smoking was minimized because "more research was needed." The same may be true of many of the food products we consume. Suffice it to say that the consumption of sugar has skyrocketed in recent years, accompanied by corresponding increases in the occurrence of obesity and diabetes. In the 1970s, one in forty-one Americans had diabetes. Today the figures are one in eleven! This is a widely reported statistic, and details of the global increase in the incidence of both types of diabetes can be found in an article written in April 2016 by Andrew Gregory (accessible at http://www.mirror.co.uk/lifestyle/health/diabetes-unrelenting-march-across-globe-7703112).

"People fall for product and health claims that are brilliantly marketed. It's hard to separate truth from fiction when the information comes from experts" (Perlmutter).

Industry continues to give us the "more research is needed" chorus with our food, medicines, microwave ovens, cordless phones, cell phones, cell antennae, and other sources of electromagnetic radiation. I recently attended a lecture by a woman named Dafna Tachover, who is passionate about warning people of the dangers of the *electromagnetic radiation* that surrounds us all. She herself is so sensitive to it that she can only live in isolated places far away from any sources of radiation. After years of being sick and nonfunctional and without getting answers from her doctors, she discovered that the radiation in her home and from the above-mentioned sources played havoc with her body. She suffered severe headaches, chest pains, nausea, insomnia, numbness in her fingers, and reduced brain function—all because of hypersensitivity to electromagnetic radiation. At the age of thirty-five, she was diagnosed with a brain tumor. She survived the tumor and is now on a mission to warn others about the dangers of the unprecedented load of electromagnetic radiation in our surroundings. Clearly, this woman's sensitivity to radiation is an extreme case, but it illustrates the potential harm that some of us are exposed to.

Information about Dafna's personal experience and research can be found on the Internet (http://ehsfighback.blogspot.co.il/search/label/English). She has researched the subject thoroughly, and reports that more than ten thousand studies have been done on the various kinds of radiation to which we are exposed. The results are reason for serious concern. Warning lights are flashing all around us in the form of unexplained fatigue, malfunctioning organs, depression, and so many other conditions that rob us of healthy lives. Dafna provides guidance on how to minimize exposure to radiation.

In the lecture I attended, Dafna showed a film called *Take Back Your Power*, which was about the health concerns of people in the United States whose homes are connected to the *smart grid*. (This is a countrywide grid that provides electricity to homes and businesses. It includes special meters inside the buildings that enable you to control your lights and electrical appliances from a distance). The film shows residents locking their properties to avoid installation of smart meters by the local authorities. However, the technicians from the electricity companies have orders to break the locks and install the meters. Anyone who refuses to have a meter installed (or disables one that was forced on him) will have no electricity in his home.

Obviously, an enormous investment has been made in the smart grid. *The adverse health effects were unexpected*, and the industry refutes any connection to people's health problems as financial interests are at stake. It says that more research is needed. Neither governmental nor medical authorities recognize *radiation hypersensitivity* as a disease, so one can understand the helplessness felt by the consumers who find themselves at risk because of exposure to high levels of radiation.

Electromagnetic fields (EMFs) are here to stay and will increase as technology advances. The installation of the smart grid is spreading to many other countries. The only solution is to reduce our exposure to electrical gadgets whenever possible, switch them off when they are not in use, and hope that industry will find ways of somehow shielding people against the full impact of radiation.

Chapter 5

Alternative Medicine and How It Works

"Alternative Medicine" is a term that refers to a range of therapeutic or preventive health-care practices that differ from standard Western medicine. They are not taught in conventional medical schools. The treatments include such modalities as acupuncture, chiropractic, reflexology, naturopathy, homeopathy, herbal medicine, among others.

Often the terms *alternative* and *complementary* medicine are used interchangeably, but the concepts are different. If the practice is used in place of modern/conventional medicine, it is considered *alternative*. If it is used together with conventional medicine, it is considered *complementary* or reciprocal and supportive. This interpretation of the term *complementary* fits in well with the belief that both the conventional and the alternative approach are relevant in the healing profession.

In the above-mentioned modalities, attention is given to the emotional state of the patient in addition to treatment of the physical ailments. For this reason, they are referred to as being *holistic* as they consider and treat the whole person.

Alternative healing methods are based on the concept of a *life force* or *vital energy* that circulates within and around all living beings, providing the energy for our bodies to function in a healthful way.

> The term *life force* or *vital energy* is not part of the scientific vocabulary. The source of this energy is unknown, and no one can create it. It cannot be measured, and much less can it be defined by a formula. Although this term does not appear in the scientific lexicon, we know that vital energy exists and most of us are ready to agree that a young athlete at the peak of his performance possesses more life force than an old, disabled and sick person. The same can be said of our thoughts. They are not quantifiable. We cannot assign them a weight, volume or color, but we don't conclude that we do not think (Tibika).

Without this vital force or *invisible intelligence*, the material part of our bodies would just be a pile of dead stuff. We can't see or touch it, but it is with us all the time.

Some people consider alternative diagnostic and healing techniques to be New Age fads not to be taken seriously. The reality is that many of these methods are ancient practices found in Eastern medicine and have been used successfully for thousands of years. In the West, more and more people are turning to these natural healing methods and mind-body therapies to solve their health problems, and increasing numbers of medical schools have started to include holistic therapies in their courses. The demand by the public has become so great that many insurance and health-care programs in Western countries now subsidize alternative/complementary therapies for their clients. "As the public is opening its eyes, medicine is opening its mind. The acceptance of different forms of healing by non-conventional medicine, such as acupuncture and homeopathy, was a first step. Now we are seeing departments of energy medicine springing up," says Dr.

Eric Pearl, a chiropractor who discovered that he was able to heal his patients of chronic conditions that conventional doctors had not been able to heal. He did it in a new way that bypassed what he had been trained to do and produced incredible results. He describes his technique in his book *The Reconnection*. The numerous invitations he receives to speak at universities and hospitals demonstrate a more open mind-set that is being adopted throughout his native United States, but it is happening in every other country as well.

Pearl believes that a change is taking place in the consciousness of health-care professionals. There is a realization by many physicians that they are not fulfilling the spirit of the dream with which they entered the profession, recognizing that there must be something more. There is now a willingness to look at it.

In the East, life force or vital energy is called *prana* (in Sanskrit) and *qi* or *chi* (in Chinese) among other names. This energy flows in channels or pathways called *meridians* that form an energy network which connects the entire physical body. This network is also referred to as our "subtle-energy system." It is called *subtle* because it cannot be detected by the five senses.

Each meridian is associated with an organ or specific part of the body. There are twelve major energy pathways that are associated with specific organs, but Chinese physiologic charts of the human body display many more and resemble complex electronic wiring diagrams. When the energy flow in a particular meridian is blocked, it indicates a decrease in vitality in the organ or region corresponding to that meridian. If the blockage is extensive it can result in suboptimal health or even illness. The techniques used in holistic medicine facilitate the flow of vital energy through the meridians, the basic principle being to create balance in the body and thus help it to heal.

The Chinese identified and mapped the meridian system more than two thousand years ago, and Chinese medicine is based on maintaining this system clear of blockages. In the healing technique of *acupuncture*, which is part of traditional Chinese medicine, special needles are inserted into the skin at specific points along the meridians to restore and regulate the flow of energy to the organ or area to be treated. A method that is similar to acupuncture but is easier to learn is *acupressure*, where pressure instead of needles is applied at the acupuncture sites. This requires less training (and may be somewhat less effective than using needles), but it is widely used and definitely produces results. Other similar techniques that stimulate acupuncture points are shiatsu massage and EFT (described in the following section). Since these techniques are noninvasive, any side effects that may occur are minimal.

There is an interesting Chinese publication that has been translated into English titled *Chinese Channel Theory*, written by Dr. Wang Ju-Yi of the China Academy in Beijing. He describes the meridian system and how it is related to the yin-yang concept and the five elements (water, earth, fire, wood, and metal). Dr. Ju-Yi writes, "The channel system is like a web which connects, integrates, and communicates among the various aspects of physiology. The channels are an integral part of the organs themselves, and they link organs to organs, and the body to the qi in the external environment." He describes the ways in which the channels are used to diagnose illnesses, including the method of pulse diagnosis. This book provides detailed explanations of the techniques used to diagnose the condition of the organs, and it also touches on nutrition.

Two other books that teach about meridians and acupressure are *Finger Pressure* by Pedro Chan and *Touch for Health* by John Thie and Matthew Thie. Both books provide illustrations of the acupressure points and diagrams of the meridians.

Although reports of acupuncture have been recorded in the West since the 1800s, it wasn't until 1974 that this method of therapy became well publicized when a reporter for the *New York Times* accompanied President Nixon on his groundbreaking trip to China. They witnessed several demonstrations of surgeries being performed without anesthetic. The only pain relief during these surgeries was provided through acupuncture. Despite many efforts to understand this, Western science has not been able to explain how it works but has had to admit that it does indeed work.

Most scientific studies of acupuncture have focused on the analgesic aspects of pain relief. It works in 70 to 80 percent of cases, which is higher than the 30 percent rate that occurs with the placebo effect (where 30 percent of people heal when given an inactive substitute such as a sugar pill instead of the real medicine). The fact that acupuncture works on animals excludes the possibility that the results obtained are due to the placebo effect.

The World Health Organization has cited more than a hundred ailments for which acupuncture treatment has been shown to be effective, including chronic pain, migraine, sinusitis, cold, flu, asthma, allergies, ulcer, gastrointestinal disorders, sciatica, arthritis, and even addictions.

Western medicine has not acknowledged the existence of the meridian system or its function. For years Western scientists have searched for the meridian system in the human body, using thermal, electronic, and radioactive methods in their studies, and the following is a summary of some of the findings to date:

a) Studies carried out in the period between 1950 to the 1970s reported that the electrical conductivity at the acupuncture sites (acupoints) is higher than the conductivity of the skin at nonacupoints. The points along the channels showed significantly more electrical conductivity than skin at nonacupoints.

b) In the 1980s, researchers injected radioactive isotopes into acupuncture points (of human subjects). They tracked the movement of the isotopes using a special gamma-ray imaging camera. Their route followed the exact same pathways of the channels described and illustrated in the ancient acupuncture charts of the human body. When the researchers inserted and twirled acupuncture needles into distant acupoints along the same tracer-labeled meridians, a change was produced in the rate of flow of the isotope through the meridian. When the researchers injected isotopes into blood vessels, the isotopes did not travel in the same manner, indicating that *meridians comprise a separate system of pathways in the body*. When injected randomly at nonacupoint regions of the skin, the radioactive tracer diffused outward from the injection site in a typical circular pattern.

c) Using infrared scanning and magnetic resonance imaging (MRI), researchers have demonstrated that communication along meridians is faster by orders of magnitude than known signaling processes of the nervous system, perhaps approaching the speed of light. Measurements of the exact speed of these energy signals through the body were hampered because of limitations of current technology.

Energy signals travel in the body at an infinitely greater speed than *chemical signals*. Based on numerous research reports, Dawson Church and Bruce Lipton (in their books *The Genie in Your Genes* and *The Biology of Belief* respectively) tell us that electromagnetic frequencies relay information at much greater speeds and at greater efficiency than the body's regulatory chemicals. Hormones, neurotransmitters, and other biologically active chemicals travel less than one centimeter per second, while energy signals travel through the energy-conduction pathways in the meridians at speeds many orders of magnitude higher.

Church explains that the insertion of the acupuncture needle into the skin creates a piezoelectric charge at the point of contact, sending an electric current through the meridian. (Piezoelectricity is described below, under the heading Energy Healing.)

Further details about the meridian system can be obtained at http://upliftconnect.com/science-proves-meridians-exist/ and http://www.eftuniverse.com/research-and-studies/articles-evidencing-the-existence-of-energy-meridians.

The Chakras

No discussion of the body's energy system can be complete without a description of the chakras. The chakras are energy centers that are connected to the endocrine system and specific organs. There are seven major chakras located along a central column from the base of the spine to the crown of the head. There are other minor chakras located at the feet, knees, hands, and many others places in the body, but this discussion focuses on the seven main ones.

The word chakra comes from the Indian language Sanskrit, where it means *wheel*. Hence, the use of the term *rotating vortex* to describe it. The concept of the chakras has its origin in the yogic and ayurvedic traditions of ancient India. *Ayurvedic medicine* is one of the world's oldest holistic healing systems, developed thousands of years ago in India, and it is known and practiced in the West. It is a complex discipline that recognizes three basic body (metabolic) types and treats disturbances in health by means of nutrition that is specific to each type, together with herbal remedies, massage, yoga, and meditation. The basic tenet is that good health depends on a balance between mind, body, and spirit.

Ayurveda (and indeed all the holistic therapies) use an integrated approach to help heal the whole person. It is believed that physical illness usually has a nonphysical origin and results from emotional disharmony. Maintaining a healthy mind and spirit helps to maintain a healthy physical body.

Many alternative therapies treat illnesses by working on the chakras to restore energy and balance in the patient. Besides their role in keeping the physical body in balance, the chakras also relate to the nonphysical or ethereal body (the aura). They thus reflect not only the physical state of the person but the emotional and mental states as well. Normally, before a disease or physical disturbance manifests in an organ, a disturbance in the corresponding chakra can be detected. A chakra that is malfunctioning or out-of-balance adversely affects the corresponding parts of the body. When the chakras are open and the energy flow is unhindered, our life force (chi or prana) flows freely through the body. The chakras are the core of an energy network that affects every aspect of the individual—physical, emotional, mental, and spiritual.

Each chakra is associated with a specific *vibration*. The lowest chakra at the base of the spine vibrates at a frequency corresponding to the red wavelength, and each successive chakra through to the crown vibrates at a higher frequency. The top chakra in the crown of the head vibrates at the highest frequency of the seven, at the violet wavelength.

Following is a brief outline of the seven chakras, giving the name, location in the body, associated body region, and corresponding color (which indicates the frequency), starting with the lowest at the base of the spine.

First chakra: called the *root chakra*; base of the spine—related to the adrenal glands, kidneys, colon, and spinal column. Color red. It is the energy center through which we experience "fight or flight." It relates to physicality, influencing our survival instinct and how we relate to money and supporting ourselves.

Second chakra: called the *sacral chakra*; lower abdomen—related to the sexual organs (ovaries in women, testes in men). It is the chakra of creativity. Color orange. It governs attitudes in relationships, sex, and reproduction.

Third chakra: called the *solar plexus chakra*; upper abdomen—related to the pancreas and governs the stomach, liver, gall bladder, and spleen. Color yellow. This is our personal power center; influences our self-esteem and self-confidence.

Fourth chakra: called the *heart chakra*; center of the chest—related to the heart, blood, circulatory system, and the thymus gland. Color green. It is our love and emotional center; influences our ability to love.

Fifth chakra: called the *throat* chakra; located at the base of the neck—related to the thyroid gland, larynx, lungs, mouth, and metabolism. Color blue. It is the center of expression and communication.

Sixth chakra: called the *third eye chakra*; located in the center of the forehead—related to the pituitary gland, autonomic nervous system, and sensory organs (eyes, nose, and ears). Color indigo. This chakra is referred to as the psychic center and influences our intuition, imagination, dreams, and ability to make decisions.

> **Seventh chakra**: called the *crown chakra*; located at the top of the head—related to the central nervous system and the pineal gland. Color violet or sometimes the combination of all colors (white light). It is referred to as the spiritual center. It relates to spirituality and links us to our higher self and the creative source.

An in-depth discussion of the chakras is provided by Richard Gerber in his book *Vibrational Medicine,* a monumental work that explains many different forms of energy healing. Gerber gives a description of the role of the chakras in our well-being. He writes that the chakras contribute subtle nutritive energy (or life force) to the body. Whereas the digestive system takes in biochemical energy in the form of physical nutrients that promote cellular growth, "the chakras, in conjunction with the meridian system take in vibrational energies that are just as integral to the proper growth and maintenance of physical life. The subtle energy currents conveyed by the chakras and meridians assist in promoting stability and organization which become manifest as physical cellular events."

Energy is taken into the body through the crown chakra at the top of the head and flows downward to the lower chakras, which distribute it to the appropriate organs and body parts. Just as white light entering a prism becomes split into the seven colors of the rainbow, in a similar fashion, the cosmic energy entering the crown chakra splits into seven vibrational levels.

> Each organ within the body has an energy frequency of its own. Organs of similar frequency tend to be clustered together in the same body region or to be linked in a special physiologic relationship. For instance, the solar-plexus chakra is connected to organs that lie in the general vicinity of the solar-plexus (stomach, pancreas, gall bladder and liver). Subtle energies distributed to these organs by

this chakra help to maintain the health and function of this aspect of digestion (Gerber).

Reflexology

Reflexology is a technique of applying pressure to specific points on the body to relieve pain and to treat health disturbances in all the organs of the body. Every organ, gland, and physiological feature has its counterpart in a reflex point on the feet, hands, and ears, all of which are considered to *mirror* the whole body.

The reflex points on the feet and hands are located at the ends of the meridians, which run along the whole body. The ears also contain points that are connected to all the organs of the body. Apart from the feet, hands, and ears, there are reflex points in other parts of the body that are used to treat specific problems. Applying pressure (using the tips of the fingers) to these points promotes energy flow through the meridians and enhances the healing of the organs located on these meridians.

In the following paragraphs, I describe the basic principles of *foot reflexology*.

The condition of the feet, namely their sensitivity or pain at a reflex point, swelling, discoloration, and dryness/moisture of the skin, enable the therapist to assess the state of health of the patient, pinpointing the origin of the imbalance that is responsible for the symptom.

The foot is divided longitudinally from the heel to the toes into five zones correspond to five zones running the length of the body from the toes to the top of the head. Treating a point in a specific zone of the foot affects all the organs that are located in the corresponding zone of the body.

The foot is also divided into transverse zones, representing the body as follows: The toes and the area just below the toes correspond to the head, neck, and shoulder girdle. The pad of the foot reflects the chest. The soft tissue of the arch corresponds to the abdomen. And the heel contains reflex points for the hip and pelvis. Reflex points may be used as alternative areas for treatment if the affected body part cannot be treated directly because of an injury.

Prior to a treatment session, the therapist gathers as much information as possible from the patient. In addition to the specific ailments, he takes into account all the factors that may be contributing to the patient's health problem. The therapist thus considers the whole person and does not isolate the symptoms. The treatment itself follows, and the therapist works on the whole foot, paying special attention to the problem areas to alleviate specific symptoms.

Reflexology treats virtually every health problem. It is a noninvasive form of therapy that improves blood circulation and stimulates the body's innate ability to heal itself by restoring the energy balance. In addition, a foot massage induces relaxation and serves as preventive therapy. The goal is to promote optimum health and well-being.

There are many excellent books on reflexology and on foot reflexology in particular. The following three books have good illustrations and explanations, and I recommend them for anyone wishing to learn more about foot reflexology: *Secrets of Reflexology* by C. McLaughlin and N. Hall, *Reflexology and Acupressure* by J. Wright, and *Feet First: A Guide to Foot Reflexology* by L. Norman. A very good book that teaches the location of reflex points over the whole body is *Body Reflexology: Healing at Your Fingertips* by M. Carter and T. Weber. Details of these publications are provided in the bibliography.

EFT (Emotional Freedom Technique)

EFT is sometimes called "acupuncture without needles." In this technique the fingertips are used to tap lightly on certain meridian points used in acupuncture. At the same time, the patient mindfully tunes in to the "problem" that he wishes to treat, describing it in words. A link between mind and body is thus established.

The method targets emotional issues, sometimes bringing to the surface forgotten events and revealing them as the cause of the present physical problem. Since many illnesses are emotionally induced, profound *physical healing* occurs when the emotional memory or trauma is relieved. EFT also overcomes the *emotional* disturbance itself, releasing phobias and issues such as anger, fear, guilt, and remorse, thus enabling the patient to achieve a relaxed state. For these reasons, EFT is referred to as energy psychology. It works quickly and without side effects.

Scientific studies and case histories support the efficacy of EFT in treating pain and a wide range of physical health problems as well as insomnia, anxiety, depression, cravings, and PTSD (post-traumatic stress disorder).

The technique includes a simple self-assessment procedure that enables the patient to determine whether the problem has been cleared with that session or whether further work is required. The relief brought about by EFT is long-lasting, as shown when subjects are interviewed months after being cured.

EFT is easy to learn. A person can either consult an EFT practitioner or apply the technique himself. The founder of EFT, Gary Craig, has been generous in sharing his method with the world. On the Web, he provides *The EFT Manual* free of charge. The manual has pictures that show the location on the body of the points used in tapping, and it teaches the principles and method of EFT. People all over the world are learning to use EFT and deriving great health benefits from it. Its popularity has spread by word of mouth, and there have been more than half a million downloads of the manual. The manual, teaching DVDs, personal stories, and much more can be downloaded at www.emofree.com.

EFT evolved from the work of psychologist Dr. Roger Callahan, who created the concept of tapping and originated the technique called *Thought Field Therapy* (TFT), which is also widely used. The theory behind TFT is that our thoughts and memories have their own "thought fields" that sometimes suffer disruption in the flow of energy. Such a disruption expresses as a negative emotion or *charge*. Tapping eliminates the charge from the thought field, neutralizing the associated emotion.

Callahan listed the following basic points regarding this therapy:

- Limiting emotions (like anger, fear, and guilt) simply vanish when certain meridian points are tapped.
- The flow of energy through our bodies has a polarity.
- Reversal of this polarity (called psychological reversal) impedes healing.
- Tapping corrects psychological reversal, allowing the relief of emotional disturbances.

TFT is well explained in www.tfttapping.com and www.rogercallahan.com, and in the book *Tapping for Life* by Janet Thomson.

EFT and TFT are often referred to as meridian-based therapies. Both have demonstrated the ability to heal psychological conditions in very short periods of time—conditions that normally take many months or years to treat with conventional psychology and psychotherapy. EFT is simpler to learn, and it is now used widely by doctors, psychotherapists, social workers, and other medical professionals.

Scientist and author Dawson Church promotes EFT as one of the most successful psychological self-help techniques ever developed. In his book *The Genie in Your Genes*, he describes the method in detail, explains how it works, and provides numerous case histories and research reports. Information about this author and his work on EFT can be found at www.eftuniverse.com.

Energy Healing

Since the holistic forms of healing mentioned previously involve energy flow through the body, they fall under the term *energy healing* or *energy medicine*.

For thousands of years, long before Western scientists discovered the laws of physics, Asian medicine has honored *energy* as the principal factor contributing to health and well-being.

We now know that all matter is a form of energy based on Einstein's famous equation $E = mc^2$, where energy (E) equals mass (m) times the speed of light (c) squared.

The speed of light (c) is a constant. In other words, energy and mass are interconvertible. Einstein considered energy and matter to be so deeply entangled that it is impossible to consider them as independent elements.

Gerber explains,

> Albert Einstein proved to scientists that energy and matter are dual expressions of the same universal substance – a

primal energy or vibration of which we are all composed. Healing the body through manipulation of this basic vibrational or energetic level of substance can be thought of as vibrational medicine. The recognition that all matter is energy forms the foundation for understanding how human beings can be considered dynamic energetic systems.

This principle is further explained by Lipton (2005). "Numerous processes of cellular activity such as protein synthesis, cell division, hormone secretion and nerve growth and function, to name just a few, are regulated by specific frequencies and patterns of electromagnetic radiation." Lipton lists the references to this research in his book *The Biology of Belief.* He tells us that although all this information has been published in some of the most respected biomedical journals, these revolutionary findings have not been incorporated into the medical school curriculum. "In our material world, the invisible energy realm is the primary shaper of our lives" (Lipton).

A form of energy that cannot be seen but is an integral part of the body is *electricity.* The body itself is an electrical system.

Electricity is the foundation of both ancient and modern medicine. Electric treatments are used to regulate rhythmic disturbances of the heart, and electric shocks are still applied to patients suffering psychiatric illnesses such as severe depression. Applying an electric current to bone fractures reduces the time needed for the fractures to heal.

Both the heart and the brain generate their own electromagnetic fields. The heart's electrical field as measured with an electrocardiogram (ECG) is sixty times stronger than that of the brain as measured with an electroencephalogram (EEG). The heart has the largest electromagnetic field of any organ or region of the body (www.heartmath.org).

***

One way of generating electricity is by applying pressure to certain materials that have the ability to transform *mechanical stress* into *electrical energy*. Electricity that is generated in this way is called *piezoelectricity*, which occurs in the physical world as well as in biological systems.

Piezoelectricity literally means "pressure electricity," as illustrated by a common application of this phenomenon—the gas-lighting mechanism in our gas cookers. Pressing a button on the lighter causes a ceramic element to be struck. In response to this mechanical stress, the ceramic material, which is piezoelectric, produces an electric spark that ignites the gas in the burner.

Piezoelectricity was discovered in 1880 by the Curie brothers, who showed that different types of crystals generate electric currents when subjected to mechanical stress. Quartz crystals display this property. When a quartz crystal is subjected to mechanical pressure, it produces an electrical charge. Quartz crystals are used in many electronic devices, such as digital watches, cell phones, microphones, television remote controls, sonar instruments, among others.

Quite recently, in the mid-twentieth century, scientists began to recognize that special types of fluidlike crystals (liquid crystals) exist, and they possess some of the properties of solid quartz. They have a structure that is partly crystalline and partly fluid. The molecules in liquid crystals tend to flow like liquids, but they maintain their alignment and order like solids.

Such crystalline arrangements are very common in living tissues. These liquid crystals have piezoelectric properties. They generate electricity when compressed or stretched. For example, when bone or cartilage is compressed or a tendon is stretched, electric pulses are created.

In the 1960s, it was established that the body's *connective tissue* generates electricity in response to mechanical stress. Connective tissue is composed of insoluble collagen fibers embedded in a gel-like ground substance. The fibers occur in an ordered crystalline arrangement. Collagen is found in bones, muscles, skin, and tendons. It helps to form a fibrous network, providing support, strength, and a degree of elasticity. Connective tissue joins all the structures of the body and even connects with the cytoskeleton within the cells.

Connective tissue exhibits piezoelectric properties.

Since many of the techniques used in *energy medicine* apply pressure at specific points, they fall under the term *bodywork* (e.g., deep tissue massage, shiatsu, reflexology, and EFT). They work on the soft tissues of the body and are believed to affect healing by generating an electric field. The highly organized crystalline organization is believed to be the medium through which healing electric current is transmitted.

In his book *The Genie in Your Genes*, Dawson Church explains that the role of piezoelectricity in our body is essential in the healing process. He writes that information is continuously flowing through the body in the form of electromagnetic currents, some of which are piezoelectrically generated. "Any kind of mechanical stimulation of the body creates piezoelectricity. This includes a soothing massage and a not-so-pleasant banging of your shin against a table. Both of these experiences create a piezoelectric charge in the cells surrounding the point of contact, and a current that travels along the most conductive channel within the body."

It is believed that movement of the body also generates piezoelectricity by virtue of the tensions and compressions inherent in routine movement.

I have included these details as they provide an explanation of how energy medicine works and possibly suggest its connection with the meridian network in the body. Further information on this subject can be obtained in the publications of James Oschman, author of a groundbreaking series of articles on *healing energy* published in the *Journal of Bodywork and Movement Therapies*. Information about Oschman's publications, work, and courses can be found at www.bodywork-res.com, and excerpts of his writings are presented at www.somatics.de under the title "Readings on the Scientific Basis of Bodywork and Movement Therapies." James Oschman tells us, "Energy is basic to everything—light, heat, sound, gravity, pressure, electricity, and magnetism – energies that surround and penetrate us. But energy has been left out of medicine, which has used tunnel vision for hundreds of years." Two books that Oschman has written on healing energy (which I have not read) are *Energy Medicine: The Scientific Basis,* and *Energy Medicine in Therapeutics and Human Performance*. More information can be obtained at www.energymedicineuniversity.org/faculty/oschman.html.

***

Having sung the praises of alternative healing methods in this chapter and despite my belief in the holistic approach, I want again to acknowledge the need for conventional Western medicine in our lives. In the words of Eric Pearl, who uses most unconventional methods in his healing practice, "The strength of conventional medicine lies in two basic arenas: first-aid and crisis-care. In a medical crisis such as a serious accident, there is no one more appropriate than paramedics and medical doctors to handle bleeding and broken bones. Once I'm safely stabilized, then let's talk about chiropractic, homeopathy, nutrition and other forms of healing. This would be the more appropriate time to give your body the chance to heal itself."

Ditto for a heart attack. Give us the above-mentioned practitioners … and fast!

Pearl believes that in most cases, if we rush to the doctor at the first sign of an imbalance and start medicating and masking our symptoms from the onset, things may get so bad that our situation may degenerate to the point where we're no longer able to get back to being 100 percent.

On a personal note, my own life was saved by our family doctor when I was five months old. According to my parents, I went from very painful crying that lasted a long time to being quiet as though the pain had subsided. They did not like the sudden silence, and they called the doctor. He diagnosed my condition as intussusception and rushed me to hospital, where immediate surgery corrected the problem. I relate this story to emphasize my belief in and respect for the medical profession despite what is written in chapter 4 regarding the less than perfect state of the medical industry.

***

In Summary, I would like to list the differences between Western and Eastern medicine as follows:

- Western medicine treats *organs*. Eastern medicine treats the *whole person*, including emotional states.

- Western medicine treats *symptoms* of disease. Eastern medicine seeks to eliminate the *cause* of the disease.
- Western medicine focuses on *disease*. Eastern medicine focuses on *maintaining and promoting wellness.*
- Western medicine uses synthetic *drugs* to suppress the symptoms of an illness. Eastern medicine uses *energy work, nutrition, and herbal remedies* to restore balance once an illness has manifested.

***

A physician who received his training in conventional medicine, David Cumes, admits in his book *The Spirit of Healing*,

> As Western physicians, we are trained to fix the problem at a mechanical level; often we fail to appreciate that something is happening on a deeper level. Even if we do appreciate it, we do not have the time to delve into it more thoroughly and exorcise the cause, as a shaman might. If doctors are to be more successful in treating their patients, they should not discount intuitive information in favor of hard facts, but use both to good effect.

This reminds me of the best seller by Brandon Bays titled *The Journey*, in which she describes how she eliminated a tumor the size of a basketball in her abdomen. She refused surgery and instead underwent mind-body therapy, which involved massage and guided imagery to collapse a traumatic childhood memory. Thanks to this therapy and a raw food diet, the tumor disappeared completely in seven weeks, a fact that was confirmed by an ultrasound examination. The doctor who had insisted on surgery could not relate to the method Bays used to treat/cure the tumor. She wanted only *facts*, and dismissed the emotional journey that Bays had experienced. "She had a total lack of interest in my healing journey," writes Bays.

She concludes that doctors go into the healing profession to help people heal, but somewhere along the line, they forget that people are not just their bodies. The emotional shifts that had taken place inside Bays were every bit as real as the physical shifts that followed as a direct result. "We have bodies, minds and emotions, but most importantly what we are, is a soul – something that can't be touched, tested or surgically removed."

Another case that illustrates the profound influence of the mind and the emotions on the body is described by Dr. Cumes. He had a young female patient who had made repeated visits to the emergency room because of her problem with recurrent urinary retention (inability to empty the bladder). He was called in as the consultant urologist to evaluate the problem.

Cumes observed that there was no obstruction. The patient did not have diabetes and was not taking any drugs that might have suppressed bladder function. She fell into the category of so-called psychogenic urinary retention, which was thought to be a hysterical type of event in response to severe stress.

The patient did not admit to any current stress or difficulties in her life, but it was later learned from her psychiatrist that sexual abuse was a significant factor in her past history. Cumes concluded that since the urinary and genital systems are closely connected anatomically, physiologically, and emotionally, the trauma of sexual abuse and the ensuing psychopathology could easily result in recurrent episodes of urinary retention. "Anyone obsessed with the body only is missing the bigger picture of health. Body, mind and spirit must work in harmony and balance for healing to take place" (Cumes).

In our world today and especially in the West, most of the elderly lack physical well-being. Modern medicine does an excellent job of extending our life span into the eighth and even ninth decade, but it is not so good at keeping us healthy until the end of our days. Most old people live in bodies that are not healthy. They are overweight, walk with difficulty, and suffer pain. Such degeneration of the body is caused by lack of exercise and a lifetime of exposure to harmful substances in our food and environment. We get weighed down by financial worries, unhappy relationships, and unquiet minds. It seems that most elderly people take large numbers of pills daily—medications to treat chronic illnesses, such as diabetes, high blood pressure, heart disease, kidney disease, arthritis, or dementia. These common illnesses cause us to grind almost to a halt long before the end. Because we see this all around us, we actually expect to follow the same path!

I believe it doesn't have to be this way. It is normal to slow down as we age, but the body has an innate capacity to restore itself. Even in old age, wounds heal, colds and flus pass, and the immune system can deal with unwelcome intruders. We need to maintain our vitality with physical activity, mental activity, and soul food. Each person can find his own way to create balance and assist his inner healer to maintain a healthy body.

Spending time in nature restores body and mind. Cumes, who received his medical training at my alma mater in South Africa, encourages us to tap nature's healing powers to overcome the "soul loss" that occurs with our hectic lifestyles. Cumes says there is no medical text today that describes the condition of soul loss. Yet this affliction may be the foundation for many of the maladies we see in our modern world. He studied ancient shamanic techniques by living with the San Bushmen of the Kalahari and other shamanic cultures of Africa and Peru. From their practices he learned that "bodily treatments alone are not always effective for true holistic healing. The spirit must be treated too."

Since Cumes studied modern Western medicine, he knows from firsthand experience what medical students go through during their difficult training, which is followed by the tensions of medical practice. Present-day doctors experience intolerable stress caused by the "dreaded Ms" – namely, managed care, malpractice, Medicare and other insurance programs which lead to loss of autonomy for physicians. Add to this a mortgage and a marriage that has become dysfunctional because of all the stress, and we have physician burnout, which Cumes says has reached epidemic proportions in the United States. A telltale sign of physician burnout is the inability to be sympathetic to the patient's plight. "The physicians of today—because of the previously mentioned forces working against them—are wounded to some degree, and this wound may be hidden from their awareness. Physicians need to restore and replenish themselves for their own sake and the sake of their patients."

Having studied other cultures that live in balance with nature, Cumes offers a new paradigm for wellness that blends Western medicine with the *curative power of the wild*, namely intimate contact with nature. It can be a powerful way to achieve balance and healing.

We should bear in mind that being in the outdoors and in contact with the earth is our natural state of being. Instead, most of us (city dwellers) spend our days cooped up indoors surrounded by concrete, artificial light, and radiation from electronic devices. Then we go home to more of the same. Is it any wonder that many of us feel out of sorts most of the time?

> Nature is not only smarter than we think.
> Nature is smarter than we can think.
>
> —Ken Wilbur, philosopher and author

Part 2

Mental Well-being

Introduction to Mental Well-being

First, a few words about the one thing we all spend our lives pursuing—*happiness.*

Those of us who live in the developed countries have all the creature comforts we need, yet happiness eludes us. Why don't our pampered lifestyles and all the stuff we own bring us happiness? Modern people tend to live in the "I'll be happy when …" mode. This is largely the result of our being bombarded daily by hundreds of advertisements telling us what we need to acquire in order to be happy. As psychotherapist Ted Kuntz tells us, "The truth is that we have everything we need right now, to be happy. It is time to stop postponing our happiness."

Of course, there are many reasons for feeling unhappy. In his book *Peace Begins with Me*, Dr. Kuntz describes how he spent years in anguish as a result of his son's illness, which was caused by the toxic effects of a vaccination he received at the age of five months. For years he told himself, "I'll be happy when my son stops seizing." He thought that because his son's medical condition was outside his control, his happiness was outside of his control. One day when arriving home from work and being greeted as usual by the face of his young son happily waiting for him at the window, he heard the question, "When your son looks out the window at you, what does he see?"

"In that brief moment of reflection I realized that my son saw a father who was angry and afraid, a father who was anxious and agitated, a father who refused to accept his own child the way he is. In this moment of clarity, I knew my son deserved better. That day I made a commitment."

Dr. Kuntz committed to doing whatever it took to become more peaceful, joyful, and happy. He committed to love the son he had rather than the son who existed in his imagination—the healthy, normal child who existed before the onset of the seizures. His journey in search of peace led him to the understanding that his happiness was not dependent on his son's health or on acquiring things or getting a job, retiring, getting married, getting divorced, or winning the lottery. He learned that his *thoughts and his interpretation of events* were the determining factors in his happiness and not the events themselves. We may think that a cause of unhappiness is *stress*. We all experience stress. It is a fact of life. But *distress* sets in as a result of the meaning/interpretation we assign to the events in our lives. Different people can respond to the same event with laughter, anger, or joy, depending on the meaning that each person assigns to the event. In other words, distress originates and exists in the mind rather than being a direct effect of the stressful event itself.

There is a delightful Zen story that illustrates how the mind influences our state of being. A peasant was summoned to his master's house. At the end of the meeting the master gave him soup to eat, but just as the peasant was about to drink it, he noticed a small snake in his bowl. Not wanting to offend his master, he drank it anyway, and within a few days, he fell so ill that he was brought back to the house.

The master took him in and gave him some medicine in a small bowl. Just as the peasant was about to drink the medicine, he noticed another snake in the bowl. This time he pointed it out and complained that this was the reason he was sick in the first place. The master burst out laughing. He pointed to the ceiling from which hung a large bow and told the peasant, "It is the reflection of the bow that you are seeing. There is no snake at all." The peasant looked again, and sure enough, there was no snake in his bowl, only a reflection. He left the house without taking the medicine and regained his health that same day.

This brings us to the subject of the power of our subconscious mind. Once the subconscious mind has accepted a belief or idea, whether true or not, it will feed us thoughts to support that belief. It can make us ill or healthy, depending on the kinds of thoughts that we provide it with through our *conscious mind*. This concept is well explained by authors who are well versed in the field of "mind power" (Kehoe, 1996; Murphy, 1982; Silva, 1977).

***

There is a popular saying that goes as follows:
Watch your thoughts. They become words.
Watch your words. They become actions.
Watch your actions. They become habits.
Watch your habits. They become character.
Your character is your destiny.
(Lao Tzu, philosopher and father of Taoism)

***

A nice example of how our thoughts and beliefs manifest in the physical realm is given by Dawson Church in his book *The Genie in Your Genes*. He quotes a Harvard study that examines the difference between physical exertion, and physical exertion plus belief. The researchers recruited eighty-four maids who cleaned rooms in hotels.

The sample was divided into two groups. One group heard a brief presentation explaining that their work qualifies as good exercise. The other group did not. Over the next thirty days, the women who had heard the presentation perceived themselves to be getting more exercise than they had indicated before. Measurements taken after a month showed that their bodies had changed significantly. Blood pressure, weight, body-fat percentage, body mass index, and waist-to-hip ratio all dropped. This change occurred in just one month and followed one brief session in which the researchers exposed the women to new beliefs about their physical activity.

"Imagine the effect of the background music of our own self-talk, running in a continuous loop in our heads for many hours a day as we perform our daily routines. Making even small changes in the program can lead to significant changes in our health" (Church).

Consciously, supply your subconscious mind with positive thoughts!

"Make sure the thoughts you habitually think are based upon what you want to see happen in your life. Train yourself to think thoughts of success, happiness, health, and prosperity" (John Kehoe).

This does not come easily to most of us. It takes *awareness* of our state of mind and the ability to replace negative thoughts with positive ones. It helps if we get busy on an activity that we enjoy and if possible, change our immediate environment (moving to another room for example). This helps to distract the mind from the negative state.

We can complain because rose bushes have thorns, or
We can rejoice because thorn bushes have roses.

—Abraham Lincoln

Until quite recently, it was thought that we were entirely at the mercy of our genetic heritage. Today, with the new science of epigenetics, we understand that our well-being depends largely on the *chemical environment* we offer our cells.

This is well explained by Bruce Lipton who formulated the concept of epigenetics. Through his research in cell physiology and behavior, Lipton revealed the role of the cell's environment in regulating gene activity. Not only do the foods and liquids that we ingest directly affect the chemistry of our cells, but the cellular environment is also influenced by our thoughts and emotions through their effect on the biochemistry and the subtle energy of our bodies. For example, fear or stress result in the production of hormones and other substances that are very different from those produced when we are in a relaxed state.

Epigenetics emphasizes that we are not victims of our heredity as determined by our genes.

The studies quoted by Lipton show that only 5 percent of cancer and cardiovascular diseases can be attributed to heredity. "Ninety five percent of breast cancers are not due to inherited genes. The malignancies in a significant number of cancer patients are derived from environmentally-induced epigenetic alterations and not defective genes."

Since the body is affected by the mind, it responds to what is going on in the mind. Thoughts and emotions that are uplifting, such as love, peace, and compassion, produce vibrations that are different from the vibrations produced by thoughts and emotions of anger, hatred, and revenge.

Mental well-being affects our physiology, and consequently, it influences the health of the body.

Chapter 6

Relationships

How do you expect mankind to be happy in
pairs when it is so miserable separately?

—Peter De Vries

I like the introductory quote because it emphasizes the fact that we need to be *whole* in order to have a fulfilling relationship with another person. The adage that in a relationship the two sides *complete* each other doesn't hold. We cannot expect another person to *fill in* for our inadequacies because he will come with his own baggage and deficiencies. After all, he is human. If he, too, expects you to make him complete, then you will end up with huge gaping holes in the relationship. Interpersonal relationships present us with challenges that are best met when the participants are mature and in a state of wholeness and inner peace. This is the ideal state that few of us achieve.

I believe the quality of every relationship depends largely on the manner in which we communicate with each other. So often we unconsciously allow our emotions to surface and color our speech when we communicate with friends and loved ones.

Relationships of various kinds (parent-child, love partners, friends, employer-employee) occupy most of our time and energy. We need to develop something that most of us lack—*good communication skills.*

Living with another person is not easy. Since everyone is the result of his own individual upbringing, no two people do things the same way or have exactly the same beliefs or interests. Sooner or later, challenges arise, and it takes a lot of patience and respect for the relationship to make it work.

Regarding *love relationships,* the following sound advice is "old hat," repeated in many different sources but not always followed. It is important *how* one approaches the other person when a difficult issue arises. Make eye contact, maintain an open heart (if possible), and tell your partner, "There is something important I need to say." It is the attitude you come with, the words you use, and the care you take not to make the other person wrong.

The person cannot know what you need unless you tell him. Use words that open him, not words that will close your partner down. Get rid of old horrible habits like expressing requests as demands. When we are stressed and tired, what normally slips out of our mouths is something like "You didn't clean up the kids' mess as you agreed to do. You're a lazy slob!" Instead, with awareness of your state of frustration, you could say, "I came home tired to a messy house, and I am very annoyed. You didn't keep your side of our agreement to clean up after the kids." These are "I" statements that clearly describe the problem (facts) and describe how you feel. They express your needs and the consequences when they are not met, and they are much more effective because they do not blame or cause hurt—two things that send the other person into defensive mode rather than cooperative mode.

Sounds easy, right? Well, it's not, mostly because of the way we respond to triggers that set us off. Knowing the theory about good communication is a good start, but then comes the practice to overcome our poor behavior and knee-jerk reactions.

New skills do not sprout overnight. Consciously, program yourself to discuss the problem wisely, using "I" statements and not blaming the other for everything. And compassionate listening won't harm either.

Listening is the greatest gift you can give someone you love.

—Thich Nhat Hanh

I think that a great piece of advice is to consciously treat your partner exactly as you would treat your best friend. Speaking kindly to a good friend comes naturally, but this is not always the case with a live-in partner. Few of us are aware of the power that nasty words have to kill good feelings and destroy a relationship.

There is a delightful book that describes different ways of communicating and the secret to understanding the kind of communication your partner needs in order to feel appreciated, loved, and happy with the relationship. *The 5 Love Languages* written by Gary Chapman explains that many relationship problems are the result of people being misunderstood because their form of communication is a mismatch for their partner/spouse. People interpret ordinary words in unexpected ways. "What makes one person feel loved is not always the thing that makes another person feel loved." For example, a husband may lovingly tell his wife how proud he is of her, while what she needs to feel loved is for him to *help with the household chores*. For her, getting help tells her that he cares and loves her. For someone else, spending *quality time together* may be what "fills the emotional tank." The other three emotional love languages are *physical touch*, *words of affirmation*, and *receiving gifts*. Chapman describes cases where one side feels extremely unappreciated and unloved, while the partner is convinced that he is genuinely expressing his love. He is, but not in the way that is required by the other side.

For some people "words speak louder than actions." They need the affirmation from the partner that he loves them, while for others physical contact speaks louder than words. I know someone for whom the simple form of physical contact, holding hands, is important. It gives her a feeling of comfort and closeness with her partner. When he forgets this simple act, she thinks that he is withholding affection and feels neglected, or even rejected—the last thing on his mind! This is an extreme case that may even seem silly, but it is very real for her, and illustrates the point.

The 5 Love Languages is a book that can be of tremendous help for anyone experiencing misunderstandings with a partner since the best of intentions can be thwarted by mismatched communication needs.

Differences of opinion on various subjects can lead to arguments. Even something that is external to the relationship itself, like politics, can cause discord between couples when there is a clash of ideals. Anna Post, spokesperson for the Emily Post Institute, describes the importance of good communication between couples with different political views, telling us that it takes a lot of patience and respect for the relationship, especially when people do not share the same political outlook. Her comments are relevant to communication on other subjects as well. "It has to do with the tone of the conversation and knowing why you are having it. It's not about what the differences are. It is how you choose to bridge them that will create a problem or make things work smoothly." It is important to know which boundaries not to push or cross. Communications experts advise us to take such conversations/arguments very carefully as no one ever wins in a battle of personal beliefs. It is essential to be respectful of each other's viewpoints.

The same advice holds for differences in religious beliefs.

Examine what truly matters in the relationship. Often it pays to keep one's mouth shut.

Speech is natural; silence is an art.

—Source unknown

There is a great need for kindness in our world. Just as harsh words or nasty actions directed at us stay with us, so too is the impact of kindness long-lasting. People who receive acts of kindness, especially when they are in distress, will always remember and are likely to do the same for others. It has a snowball effect.

There is a section in the book *Mind Power into the 21ˢᵗ Century* titled "Human: Handle with Care." The author, John Kehoe, points out that people tend to hurt others when they themselves have been wounded. When observing his own reactions, he realized that whenever he was mean or hurtful toward someone else, it was always because he himself was suffering. When someone does something unpleasant to us, we should ask what pain he might be suffering inside and then offer love and compassion for them. We don't know what fears, disappointments, or insecurities people carry within them. Remember the old saying "Don't judge a person until you've walked a mile in his shoes."

Much has been taught and written about the importance of *forgiveness* in our relationships and our lives. When we are cheated on or offended in any other way, we develop hurts and resentments that *bring us down* because of the pain they cause. Religion and psychology tell us that we must forgive our offenders, something that is not always easy to do. I will not delve into this subject. I wish only to cite the following quotation:

> Hanging on to a resentment is like drinking
> poison and hoping it will kill someone else.

—Quoted by many, original source unknown.

We are social beings. We need contact with other people. Interpersonal relationships are important to us to the point of being vital to our well-being. Some people have a greater need than others to be with people, but without a doubt, the quality of our lives depends to a large extent on the quality of our interactions with other people.

Relationships impact our mental health. They affect our moods, helping us to feel happy and optimistic when the interaction is harmonious, or to feel uneasy or even sick when the interaction is hostile.

Make time to cultivate good friendships. When we are lonely or going through a rough patch, a good friend can provide comfort and support, in addition to being part of our good times as well. And of course, we must be there for them too.

Here's a final thought to end this chapter on relationships. A loyal friend is a true blessing. Nurture your relationships. Cherish your friends. In some cases, our friends are the family we choose to be with.

Chapter 7

Parenting

Parenting is a vast topic that covers our involvement with our offspring from day one through many stages that can be broadly divided into babyhood, the toddler stage, pre-school, schooling, adolescence, young adulthood, and adulthood. Apart from the fun and pleasure of raising a child, each of these stages brings its specific challenges, the intensity of which depends on the prevailing conditions related to the child, the parents, and the home environment. Volumes have been written about each of these stages, and in this chapter I focus on the *adolescent stage* only. I present my thoughts, derived from the lessons I learned about it and the literature that helped me along the way.

I am not an expert on parenting, but I did learn some important things that are worth passing on. What I write reflects my own experiences—both as a teen and a parent. At first, the reader may assume that the information presented here is outdated since the issues that parents and children grapple with today are different from those we coped with "in my day." Every generation faces new challenges as the world around us changes, but the *needs* of both parents and children remain the same, namely to be understood, accepted, and loved.

Parenting is probably the most important thing we do in our lives and the one we are least prepared for. Even if there were courses (or university degrees) on how to parent, they wouldn't be as useful as they sound because every child and every family situation is different, and therefore, there is no one method that fits all. Each situation requires wisdom and skill on the part of the parents. Since parents always want the best for their children, we often botch things up because of too much concern with getting it right.

I start this section with beautiful words of wisdom from the book *The Prophet* by Kahlil Gibran.

> Your children are not your children.
> They are the sons and daughters of Life's longing for itself.
> They come through you but not from you,
> And though they are with you yet they belong not to you.
>
> You may give them your love but not your thoughts.
> For they have their own thoughts.
>
> You may strive to be like them, but seek not to make them like you.
> For life goes not backward nor tarries with yesterday.

If I had started writing this book twenty-five years ago, I would have focused on issues related to toddlers, the terrible-twos being known as the most stubborn age. However, having lived through and survived the longer and more challenging stage of raising adolescents, I want to focus on this stage of parenting.

When I was in my teens, my parents' main concern was to keep me safe from the opposite sex. My mother consistently disapproved of my hair and makeup, which to this day I still think were just fine and normal for my age. Smoking was a major crime both at school and in my family. Dating became an issue and the subject of enormous conflict until I won the battle in my second year at university! Alcohol was available, but I don't remember that we drank in excess. And drugs were not part of my experience or of anyone in my circle of friends.

Fast-forward to the period that my children grew up in, when the fashion for girls was skimpy blouses and ultra low-slung jeans. Girls absolutely had to expose their midriffs and other parts, in order to be *cool* like everyone else. It went so far that a male teacher at our school made repeated requests from parents to enforce a stricter dress code as he found the existing situation uncomfortable. Unlike my own school days when smoking was forbidden and would get you expelled, there was a smoking corner on the grounds in my children's school! It was illegal for stores to sell cigarettes and alcohol to children under the age of eighteen, but that didn't stop kids having access to both. On weekends alcohol flowed freely down the throats of many underage teens. In addition, the deafening noise and hostile lyrics that passed as music from their favorite heavy metal bands routinely scrambled their brains. The whole scene was very different from my experience growing up as a teen—it was quite bewildering.

Some kids were compliant while others were rebellious, some extremely so. Some parents could stay in control, but others could not. There was no single approach that worked in all cases.

The way we parent depends a lot on how and where we ourselves grew up (our parents' ways, the age gap, culture, religion, etc.). In my own parenting experience, I found myself facing not only a huge age gap but also a cultural gap, a repeat of my own upbringing. As a teen, I believed I had "problem parents." My parents grew up in a remote European village and kept their extremely conservative ideas and values when they immigrated to South Africa. They tried to impose these on me because they did not accept the local customs, which to them seemed quite decadent. They were strict and overprotective, especially with respect to dating. The concept of *boyfriend* was taboo in our house, and was meticulously avoided. Their mind-set did not exclude marriage, but unsupervised dating … heaven forbid! Since I was growing up in a different culture, I did not accept their outdated ideas, so there was plenty of conflict. Only when I was in my late teens and after they got to know my fellow students did they understand that (at least some) boys were normal, decent creatures who probably did not present a threat.

By the time I started raising my own kids, the world had changed, and dramatically so in my new country of residence, which I considered to be ultra-liberal. I caught myself repeating my parents' authoritarian approach, which I had abhorred as a teenager. It worked with one of my children but not with the other. In the latter case, it only fortified the defiant and rebellious reaction.

With time I managed to overcome my ingrained, conservative attitudes to some extent. I have no doubt that it was a difficult time for my kids as well. I comfort myself with the thought that most people have unpleasant memories from their childhood because of defective parenting and that I was not uniquely awful.

***

Based on my own experience, there is one piece of advice that I believe can save many stormy parent-teenager relationships, and that is this: Accept the fact that behavior changes radically during the teen years in the majority of children. There is nothing you can do about this. A rebellious stage seems to be programmed into our DNA as a species. It is almost as though a temporary change occurs in the brain at adolescence, leading to inexplicable behavior. Recently, I came across a book written by Dr. Frances Jensen called *The Teenage Brain. A Neuroscientist's Survival Guide to Raising*

Adolescents and Young Adults. He writes about the neurosis of the adolescent brain and states, "Functioning, wiring, capacity—all are different in the adolescent." This book provides insight into what makes our teenagers tick.

Luckily, things straighten out after a few years. We try so hard to impose our "right" ways on our teens, and most of us do this unskillfully. We criticize them continuously and try to change them to fit our view of the world. Please understand that criticism does not help. It only makes the child feel misunderstood and unsupported. It is hard not to be critical of bad behavior that can become destructive, but try to step back and remember that your teen is going through his own confused, difficult stage. He is no longer a child but does not yet have the experience of a grown-up. There are few role models that he can look up to, and his equally confused peers have a very strong influence on him. At this stage, his friends and the need to be accepted by the group become more important than parental views. The friends can range from *good kids* who mostly behave according to the norms of society to really *bad company* that can influence your child to do things that will horrify you.

This is only a phase, but it's a very important one in a young person's life.

From the authors mentioned in this chapter, I learned the following: Try to maintain a healthy level of supervision, and let your teenager know you are there for him no matter what. Always *acknowledge good behavior* when it happens, no matter how insignificant it may seem. Your approval can have a major positive effect on him, even if it only becomes obvious further down the line. Sometimes teenagers behave so badly that it is hard to love them at that moment. Don't let it show. As much as possible, try not to over-react. It is important to discuss things together without yelling, blaming, or criticizing. This is not always possible because teenagers are typically noncooperative and think that parents don't know anything. Only someone who has raised a difficult teenager can understand the helplessness that parents experience in view of the potential dangers and consequences of their child's behavior. For some parents, it is a process filled with frustration, anxiety, and desperation.

A Bit of Humor:
Teenagers! Tired of being hassled by your stupid parents?
Act now. Move out, get a job, pay your own bills,
while you still know EVERYTHING!

—Source unknown

I have placed much emphasis on the raising of difficult teenagers, but thankfully, not all teens are difficult or live dangerously, or cause their parents anguish, which is a blessing for all concerned.

I raised my children at a time and place where the approach was "the child is king." Most little princes and princesses were badly spoiled and allowed to rule the roost. In some cases, we created little monsters. Gradually, it became clear that we the parents were partly to blame and that a different approach was needed, namely more discipline like in the old days. At the time, there was a local psychologist who recommended very harsh treatment for wayward adolescents. She *broke* them into submission with no sympathy for their current condition. Desperate parents took their children to her in the hope of "fixing" them. I know one family who consulted with her, but the child didn't change because he couldn't. The fact was that he wasn't a bad kid at all. He was just different and didn't live up to his parents expectations. At the other extreme, there was a young boy in the same group of kids who was also different from the mainstream but had the good fortune to have parents who accepted his academic limitations and supported him through his struggles. They didn't force him to change. His mother had had a difficult childhood herself and therefore understood him better than *ordinary* parents would. This boy grew up without the drama and remained close to his family. He is finding his way in the world in his own time and with the support he needs. His upbringing was so much more balanced than that of his friends who were raised under constant *fixing* in the form of criticism and incessant nagging.

There are two wonderful books that I would like to mention here—*Raising Cain* (Kindlon and Thompson) and *Adolescence: The Survival Guide for Parents and Teenagers* (Fenwick and Smith). They provide guidance on how to change ineffective parenting styles and habits and how to set limits by negotiation rather than force. Consider this story by Anthony De Mello:

> I was a neurotic for years. I was anxious and fearful and selfish. Everyone kept telling me to change—my parents, teachers, even my best friend was telling me to change.
>
> As a result I felt self-conscious, resentful and trapped.
>
> Then one day, a friend said to me, "Don't change, I love you just the way you are." Those words were music to my ears: "Don't change. Don't change … I love you just the way you are."
>
> I relaxed.
>
> I came alive.
>
> And suddenly I changed!

Lawrence Keleman wrote a great book titled *To Kindle a Soul*, in which he presents an enlightening perspective to parenting. Instead of focusing only on the child and how to change him, he encourages parents to change themselves and their approach, to become good parents and teachers.

Keleman states that raising children properly guarantees nothing, emphasizing that even the most effective approaches only give a child a head start. Our children have free will, and ultimately, they will decide how to live their lives.

> We hope they will make good choices and we must do everything in our power to help, but we are not necessarily responsible for the final outcome. We need to remember that no parent or teacher is perfect. We all make mistakes— sometimes because we were never taught to handle the complexities of child-raising, and sometimes because we are fallible human beings. The real measure of parents and teachers is not whether they make mistakes, but whether they make valiant efforts to avoid repeating them (Keleman).

The following ideas regarding wise parenting come from a gem of a book by Jon Kabat-Zinn titled *Wherever You Go, There You Are.* This is a book about mindfulness, and I present here a part on parenting:

You are your children's major life teacher as much as they are your teachers, and *how* you take this role will make a big difference in their lives as well as in your own. In addition to the basic instincts for nurturing (being loving and kind) in order to do this job well, a proper guardian or guide needs patience and wisdom in abundance to pass on what is most important. Some need virtually constant mindfulness.

The best way to impart wisdom or anything else to your children is to live it yourself, embody what you most want to impart, and keep your mouth shut. The more you extol an idea or insist that your children do things a certain way, the more likely you are to turn them off. They will see your strong attachment to your view and the aggression behind your enforcing beliefs, which are only your own and not theirs.

The real teaching is almost nonverbal. For example, Kabat-Zin's children sometimes did yoga with him because they saw him doing it. Although most of the time they had more important things to do, they had some idea of what yoga was about and knew that he valued it and practiced it himself. When they want to, they'll know what it is about from doing it with him when they were little. In my own family, when out walking in nature, my brother-in-law would quietly pick up litter left behind by people touring the area. I am sure his children will, in turn, care about the environment and behave in the same way. (It certainly impressed me!)

In today's world of ever-present stimuli, information overload, and the lack of quiet time, the following words for parents from Kabat-Zin make sense: "Just being centered yourself, fully present and open and available is a great gift for your children. And mindful hugging doesn't hurt either."

Talking of hugging, a close friend of mine in his late fifties told me more than once, "My mother never hugged me." He carried this feeling of not being loved all his life! Another friend in his sixties often laments that when he was growing up, his father couldn't spend time with him (because of long workhours in the family business). To this day, the lack of contact and guidance from his father lingers as a sad memory.

These two examples may seem trivial, but they illustrate the importance of right parenting. Feeling unloved as a child remains throughout a person's life, and even at an advanced age, people remember and voice the pain from their childhood.

***

When You Thought I Wasn't Looking

When you thought I wasn't looking
You hung my first painting on the refrigerator
And I wanted to paint another.

When you thought I wasn't looking
You fed a stray cat
And I thought it was good to be kind to animals.

When you thought I wasn't looking
You baked a birthday cake just for me
And I knew that little things were special things.

When you thought I wasn't looking
You said a prayer
And I believed there was a God I could always talk to.

When you thought I wasn't looking
You kissed me goodnight
And I felt loved.

When you thought I wasn't looking
I saw tears come from your eyes
And I learned that sometimes things hurt—
But that it's alright to cry.

When you thought I wasn't looking
You smiled
And it made me want to look that pretty too.

When you thought I wasn't looking
You cared
And I wanted to be everything that I could be.

When you thought I wasn't looking
I looked …
And wanted to say thanks for all the things you did
When you thought I wasn't looking.

—Mary Rita Schilke Sill © 1980
Written for my mother, Blanche Schilke.

***

Here are some thoughts on *adolescents and the educational system*:

A growing number of children are being diagnosed as having attention deficit disorder (ADD) or attention deficit hyperactivity disorder (ADHD), and/or a learning disability. Parents and teachers find it difficult to deal with these children, and in most cases medication with drugs such as Ritalin appears to be the answer. In some cases, this quick-fix solution works, but there are alternate ways of approaching the problem, and "the pendulum is now definitely swinging in the direction of recognizing the need for non-invasive, natural and commonsense alternatives to drugs" (Carla Hannaford).

Because attention deficit disorders and learning disabilities usually lead to disruptive behavior in the classroom and poor academic performance, these conditions are sometimes misunderstood. Being in the classroom is stressful for these children, and it is well known that stress causes us to lose focus and concentration. The child becomes frustrated, loses self-confidence, and suffers low self-esteem. At the same time, the parents are at their wits' end, watching their once happy child turn into a withdrawn, rebellious, hopeless teen. Freed and Parsons have written an excellent book called *Right-Brained Children in a Left-Brained World*, in which they emphasize the many gifts and talents of children labeled as ADD, ADHD, and learning disabled. "These children are right-brain dominant and have a visual learning style. They get the whole picture right away and then fill in the details later, while other kids start with a detail, add another detail, and eventually figure out the whole pattern." They do poorly in school because educators tend to be left-brain, detail-oriented, auditory processors who view visual learners as "flawed." Unfortunately, our educational system does not acknowledge that some children have a different way of learning and teachers don't know how to teach in a different way. The kids end up feeling like losers. Some of them figure that if they can't succeed at being good, they'll be the best at being the worst, and they bask in the attention they receive for their misdeeds. The bad behavior snowballs. They become frustrated, grow to hate school, and become openly defiant. Since neither the school nor the parents understand the real problem, these kids are regarded as "juvenile delinquents in training." Quite often teenagers who are facing the above-mentioned problems are conspicuous by virtue of their appearance. They present a rough, tough outer shell by the way they dress and their hairstyles, but this is a way to hide a sensitive interior that has been wounded by the school system and by parents who misunderstand their plight. A large number of adolescents who go this route drop out of school, which by now has become nothing but a painful endurance test (Kindlon and Thompson).

Hannaford reaches the same conclusions regarding right-brained, visual learners and the stress that they experience in school. "This stress impairs learning, setting off a vicious cycle that sends grades spiraling downward." Hannaford (a neurophysiologist) treats ADD and learning disorders with movement rather than drugs. She believes that movement plays an essential role in the learning process. "My fascination with the role of movement and play in the learning process came out of the miracles I witnessed with children labeled 'learning disabled'. When working with these children I found that they were more easily able to learn when we began their learning sessions with simple, whole body integrative movements."

The fact that she herself experiences measurably greater ease in thinking, communicating, and learning motivates her to study and understand why movement enhances learning so dramatically.

"Movement is essential to learning since the body plays an integral part in all our intellectual processes and its role is not solely to carry the brain from place to place so that it can do the work of thinking." Movement awakens and activates many of our mental capacities, integrating and anchoring new information and experience into our neural networks. Hannaford's book *Smart Move. Why Learning Is Not All In Your Head,* gives technical details that relate learning to brain anatomy and function, and the role played by the body-mind connection.

A study of thirteen thousand adults and children labeled as dyslexic from three different countries reported that a specific exercise performed twice daily for ten minutes freed all participants of dyslexic symptoms within six months (Britten, 2004; cited by Hannaford).

Studies have linked inactivity to learning difficulties and have shown that participation in sports at school results in better grades. However, as we know, children nowadays spend most of their free time indoors, sitting at the computer or watching television.

It has become evident that 60 to 80 percent of learning disabilities occur in boys (Kindlon and Thompson). These authors explain that the diagnosis of learning disabilities is based on assessment of reading ability at a certain age compared with IQ at the same age. The early age at which we teach reading favors girls, who master this ability at an earlier age than boys. This puts boys at a disadvantage and makes them feel inferior. "In therapy, boys frequently describe themselves as losers or failures, even when they are developing skills at a pace that is normal for boys their age." In the United States, the private Waldorf schools don't teach reading in the early grades because "if you start teaching it any earlier, it looks as if all your boys have reading disabilities." In Norway, they believe that to start teaching reading before age eight can turn a child who is simply developmentally behind the pack into a learning disabled child. Recently, the age for reading instruction in Norway was lowered, not because it was best for the children but because of the way it "looked" internationally to begin reading instruction at such a *late* age. A child that has trouble learning to read in first grade starts to hate school. "His self-esteem goes to hell."

Today many children face a steady diet of embarrassment and anxiety throughout their elementary school years. They learn only to feel bad about themselves and to hate the place that makes them feel that way. These children are "in trouble before they even learn how to spell the word" (Kindlon and Thompson).

I have witnessed this happening at close quarters, and must agree with these authors that "the so-called crisis in education is simply the failure of our schools to identify these growing numbers of children and determine the best way to teach them. Instead of treating them as 'defective' and 'disordered,' we need to recognize their innate strengths and improve their esteem and enthusiasm for learning." These authors point out that from the cradle, children are being raised in a highly visual environment with stimulating pictures and toys in their cribs, many hours of television daily, and computer games at an early age. How can teachers compete with this, using outdated methods of teaching?

Kindlon and Thompson are both psychologists. Their guiding principle is to try to keep children's self-esteem intact while they are in school. Low self-esteem is the real risk to children's success and mental health. Once they are out of school, the world will be different. They'll find a niche where their poor spelling or the fact that they didn't read until age eight won't matter. But if a child starts to hate himself because he isn't good at schoolwork, he'll fall into a hole that he'll be digging himself out of for the rest of his life.

Right parenting takes into account the importance of nurturing and protecting the internal emotional life of the boy in your life, communicating openly without judgment. "In all our years as therapists, we have never met a boy who didn't crave his parents' love and others' acceptance and who didn't feel crippled by their absence or redeemed by their abundance" (Kindlon and Thompson).

***

Much of what appears in this chapter on parenting teenagers may seem pure common sense and obvious to some readers. I have to admit that when my children were growing up, I was ignorant of much of the information that appears in this chapter, and the approach described here was not obvious to me. I was rigid with some issues and lax with others. I made mistakes, and I wish that I could go back in time and have another chance at raising my children. Knowing what I know now, I would do some things very differently!

The ultimate truth is that we do our best at the time.

Of course, not all adolescents are rebellious or exhibit the problems described here. However, for parents facing difficulties, the guidance provided by the books mentioned in this chapter can alleviate the feeling of despair by promoting understanding and better communication, thus helping both sides survive the adolescence stage with minimal damage. Apart from the technical do's and don'ts (in setting limits, for example), these books teach us the importance of *being there* with our teens during this trying period in their lives instead of alienating them with criticism and demands that are beyond their ability to comply with. It is a time when skillful guidance is desperately needed, not only on how to communicate with your teen but also to help you to gain insight into what makes him tick.

Parents often need guidelines on how to show their love and communicate their understanding skillfully, especially in times of conflict. There are very many excellent publications apart from the ones I have mentioned in the text that I found helpful at the time my children were growing up. I am aware that more recent publications will approach the subject of parenting from a more current perspective, but I believe in the value of the older references too, as our basic emotional needs and the *essence* of the parent-child relationship remains unchanged over time. It is up to parents to bridge the gap because teens are not capable of doing it.

Here is a list of books on parenting teenagers that I recommend:

- *Manhood* by Steve Biddulph,
- *Maybe You Know My Teen* by Mary Fowler,
- *Non-violent Resistance. A New Approach to Violent and Self-Destructive Children* by Haim Omer, and
- *Nurturing Your Teenager's Soul* by Mimi Doe.

***

The only thing worth giving your children is joy.

—Rabbi Nachman of Breslov

Chapter 8

Relationships across Borders

I wish to share some thoughts on the role of interpersonal relationships on the current state of our world, which ultimately reflects the human-to-human interactions within and across borders.

Modern civilized man considers many ancient customs and practices to be primitive, and rightly so as most of them are outdated and useless or even dangerous. Take for example the practice in medicine where, until the late nineteenth century, doctors repeatedly wore the same bloodstained aprons when treating patients or performing surgery. They were ignorant of the need to avoid contamination. The concept that germs cause disease was ridiculed and discarded as nonsense by the medical profession. Invisible little creatures that can kill you—how funny! Today we know about fungi, bacteria, and viruses thanks to microscopy and advances in microbiology. I could quote other examples of primitive practices and beliefs that we reject now, but I want to focus on one that continues to this day and in some countries is considered to be necessary. I refer to the persistent, primitive way of resolving conflict through war.

Mankind's history throughout the centuries is riddled with wars. Among the reasons for the butchering of man by man are fear, greed for power, greed for territory, delusions of superiority, racism, and tribalism. There has been outright brutality in the name of religion, democracy, capitalism, communism, and revenge.

> Human ingenuity knows no bounds when it comes to killing.
> Misery, despair, monstrous stupidity on both sides.

—National Geographic documentary *Apocalypse—World War I*

The end result of war has never been a clear-cut victory over the "enemy," but a lose-lose situation with both sides suffering the destruction of people and of property. Scars are left everywhere. The men on both sides suffer the same horrors of the battlefield.

Surely, at this stage in human civilization, we should be able to handle conflict through nonviolent means by engaging in sincere dialogue to understand the problem at hand. *Any conflict that drags on endlessly indicates that the violent methods used to try to end it do not work.* There needs to be a shift in approach if there is a true intention of achieving peace. War is always ugly no matter the reason for going to war.

> Peace cannot be kept by force; it can only
> be achieved by understanding.

—Albert Einstein

I am not qualified to add anything to the countless books and articles that have been written on past and present wars. But what is clear is that violence breeds more violence, generating more animosity and hatred, not to mention the trauma inflicted on the young men who are sent to do the fighting. If dialogue does not work and a country needs to defend its people, there is advanced technology that can be used effectively instead of risking young people's lives.

Fortunately, many first-world leaders have shifted in their approach to conflict resolution. Responding to provocation with violence is no longer the default, knee-jerk reaction of the past. Diplomatic solutions rather than military invasions are becoming the first option. Aggression by nations against their neighbors is now labeled as *nineteenth century acts in the twenty-first century.* Enlightened leaders want to end wars, but not through war. Other forms of punishment for perverse leaders and militant groups are available, striking where it hurts most, namely economically. Sanctions and trade boycotts are not new but are now being used as a first option instead of violence (e.g., North Korea and Iran).

There is a new consciousness in the civilized world. Today there are courses and even university degrees on conflict resolution that exclude war. There hasn't been a world war for seventy years, and in most of Europe, countries that battled one another for centuries are now united. They have dropped their borders and even share a common currency. Unfortunately, there are still many trouble spots in the world, and there have been many terrible wars since World War II (Korea, Cambodia, Vietnam, Yugoslavia, Rwanda, Congo, North and Eastern Africa, Middle East, Ukraine, and others).

The planet is not free of violence yet. Yes, the butchering continues, but most of the conflicts are occurring within national borders. Much of the violence we see today involves conflicts along ethnic lines, civil wars, uprisings against tyrant leaders, and attempts to overcome guerrilla incursions.

> Future generations will look back and identify
> this time as the Barbaric Era.
>
> —Kryon

The good news is that there are bold people who meet with the enemy in an attempt to bridge the gap through dialogue and nonviolence. Such men of peace were active in Northern Ireland during the peace process there and in South Africa toward to end of the apartheid regime. There is a name for such heroic people. They are called civil peacemakers. They are private citizens who initiate unofficial communication with representatives of the other side to pave the way to conflict resolution. This phenomenon has been researched by Lior Lehrs, who states, "The peace-makers phenomenon is a part of an ever-growing international trend of civil, unofficial diplomacy that goes beyond the issue of conflict resolution and focuses mostly on issues like human rights, environmental protection and arms control" (article May 17, 2014, in www.ynetnews.com).

These ordinary citizens try to foster peace by dropping the "fear of the other" mind-set. They care enough to make time and effort to express their concern by participating in public protests, peace marches, and rallies. As Bruce Lipton says, "Peace happens through people, not through governments. Each one of us must create peace." There are hundreds of small groups and large organizations that work toward peace in troubled areas. People are reaching out, wanting to share their understanding of the other's pain and frustration, wanting to reconcile their differences.

> If you want to make peace with your enemy,
> you have to work with your enemy.
> Then he becomes your partner.
>
> —Nelson Mandela

I acknowledge that what I am saying about war is an oversimplification. I don't have the foresight or the ability to end the conflicts currently taking place in many countries. Nor does anyone else. I just want to point out the futility of using violence to deal with conflict. We have been doing this for centuries, and it is time to find a better way.

> Definition of Insanity:
> Doing the same thing over and over again
> and expecting a different result.
>
> —Albert Einstein

***

Thanks to a change in human consciousness, countless people today—individually and in groups—are actively pursuing ways of ending the conflict situations in their countries. They understand that the use of force seldom brings lasting peace. With the exception of small pockets of fanatic extremists, those who see war as the solution to war are now in the minority.

In many conflict areas of the world, it is the women who are taking part in activities that reach across the political divide. One of the peace-building organizations that I mention here is Women Wage Peace. It consists of Israeli and Palestinian women who come together to bridge the abyss of misunderstanding and mistrust that foment animosity. One of their mottos is "The price we pay for war is much greater than the price we would pay for peace." There are many, many other groups of peace activists. These people are tired of war and the phony efforts of their leaders to achieve peace, especially since all they have achieved is the escalation of hostility and increased suffering for all.

Ordinary citizens, especially young people, are seeing through the politicians' stale stories and power games. Today, thanks to the Internet, everybody is talking to everyone else within and across borders. Young people are forging links and friendships with their counterparts in "enemy" territory. They are discovering that "*the other*" has the same needs and hopes, and is not much different from themselves.

I am hopeful that today's young people will find innovative ways of solving the endless conflicts that the older politicians are incapable of resolving. May they realize the potential for peace when they become the leaders of the future.

***

When discussing the state of our world and the hope for peace, one cannot ignore the new threat from relatively small groups of extremists who are performing barbaric acts against humanity. These groups operate in the Middle East and Africa. They butcher anyone who does not conform to their stream of Islam, including their own Muslim *brothers*. They are adding to the refugee crisis in the Middle East and Europe in addition to exporting their terror to other countries. In short, they are terrorizing the world.

Remember Al-Qaeda? Who would have thought that things could get worse?

The above-mentioned groups display a different kind of savagery from that experienced throughout man's sad history. It is captured on camera, and the full horror of it is brought to our screens almost daily—unlike the horrors of the past, which were hidden from view.

The previously mentioned groups and others are causing the number of persons displaced by conflicts to grow at an alarming rate. In mid-2016, UN agencies reported that the number of forcibly displaced persons worldwide is 65.3 million. It is the first time in the organization's history that the threshold of sixty million has been crossed (www.unhcr.org/news/latest/2016/6/).

The refugee drama is turning out to be bigger and more complex than at first anticipated, and no one can foretell how it will end.

The conflict and insecurity are preventing food aid reaching the displaced people. In May 2017, international aid agencies estimated that twenty million people face starvation in the very near future in Nigeria, Somalia, Sudan and Yemen alone.

Chapter 9

Mindfulness Meditation

For many of us, life is a constant battle against the clock. It leaves us no time to see the roses, let alone to stop and smell them. We don't have time to give enough attention to our children or to make lasting friendships or to enjoy the benefits of loving relationships.

I am reminded that in the old days most household chores were done manually until gradually, marvelous time-saving machines became indispensable in every home—washing machines, vacuum cleaners, dishwashers, food processors. How amazing to have, at the press of a button, a machine that does a heavy chore for you. The same goes for calculators, word processors, cars, high-speed trains.

Have all these amazing inventions given us more leisure time? It seems not, as we are constantly *running* and live in a state of time deprivation and often sleep deprivation, and we are not exactly happy about it. We strive constantly to pack more and more activities into our already full schedules. Not only are our bodies in a constant state of *doing*, but our minds are also normally lost in thought and hardly present, not really connected with what is happening here and now. The simple truth is that we are missing out on our lives. We need to set time aside for just *being*.

Looking at the plight of women (in particular) in contrast to bygone days when mothers stayed home raising the children and doing household chores, now these tasks are squeezed in at the end of a full workday. Weekends are often spent catching up on shopping for food and doing the laundry. Hey, where is there time to rest, to just be? Don't misunderstand me. I am not suggesting that women should stay home. That would be terribly frustrating and a waste of excellent brain power. But from my own experience, I know that even if she is fortunate enough to have a husband/partner who helps around the house, it is the woman who carries the load of running the home while augmenting the family income and striving to develop a career. I remember standing in the checkout line in a supermarket at about 8:30 one evening, feeling tired, and observing the look of exhaustion on other shoppers' faces. I thought, *Why do we do this to ourselves? The workday ended a few hours ago and we are still working! It seems we don't know when to stop doing things.*

I want to introduce the subject of *mindfulness meditation* and how it can help us to overcome our state of daily stress.

In the book *The Genie in Your Genes*, author Dawson Church explains that apart from relaxing the body and quieting the mind, "the benefits of meditation are so numerous, and the subject of so many studies, that it's hard to know where to start." Church mentions recent studies by researchers at the University of Wisconsin that show that mindfulness meditation produces a significant rise in a variety of antibodies and blood cells associated with increased immune function. This new crop of studies shows that it measurably improves the body's ability to resist disease and the effects of stress. Church quotes Dr. R. Dozor of the Integrative Health Clinic (Santa Rosa, California), "Meditation – all by itself – may offer more to the health of a modern American than all the pharmaceutical remedies put together."

Neuroscientist Richard Davidson compared EEG recordings of brain activity and PET scans during meditation of novice versus experienced meditators. He found that the experienced meditators had more brain activity in the areas linked to positive emotions such as happiness and showed greater increases in gamma waves, which are involved in attention, memory, and learning (cited by Church).

The profoundly positive effect of mindfulness meditation on the brain is described by Mark Williams (clinical psychologist) and Danny Penman (biochemist).

> The new science of brain imaging means that we can watch as critical networks in the brain become activated. Recent scientific advances allow us to see the parts of the brain associated with such positive emotions as happiness, empathy and compassion becoming stronger and more active as people meditate. As this happens, unhappiness, anxiety and stress begin to dissolve leaving a feeling of reinvigoration (Williams and Penman, 2011).

In his delightful book *The Secret Power Within*, Chuck Norris, winner of several black belts and world champion in the martial arts, and also renowned for his films, describes the philosophy behind all the martial arts and how it relates to Zen. (Zen can be defined as a branch of Buddhism that offers meditation and understanding of one's essential nature as the best way to achieve enlightenment.) In a chapter titled "Calming the Moving Mind," Norris writes,

> The alarm goes off and you wake up; the phone rings and you answer; you pause too long at an intersection and the driver behind you honks. All day long bells, whistles and horns prod us on, keep us moving toward the timely completion of each chore or task. Even in moments of relative silence, our minds rush ahead, checking off the To Do list.

What is the real source of the rush? If you look, you'll see that the movement and rush belong to the city, or the office, or the freeway; the stress and the constant push come from the telephones and the clocks and computers. They do not come from you. If you agree to respond to each impulse then you too will become part of the stress. But nothing obliges you to do so. You can't slow the city, but you can take control of your life and manage the speed with which it moves. That control begins with yourself, with small matters, the trivial everyday things of your life. If you can control the small things, you'll be better able to control, even to master, the large and important matters that come your way and add stress to your life.

Finding private time is essential for everyone, even children. The Zen masters understood this long ago and from this understanding they developed meditation, which enables the individual to introduce order and calm into the chaos of life. A calm mind is the real secret to success under stress, because a mind that is not calm will fail to perceive correctly. When you are calm, you can separate and examine your fears and perceptions.

Every meditation tradition involves daily practices that help to focus a scattered mind. Our minds tend to flit from thought to thought, and it can be difficult to maintain concentration. In meditation there are various techniques that help us to focus the mind. A commonly used technique is to focus on something that is always with you—*your breath*. In the words of Williams and Penman, "You cannot take a breath for five minutes ago, or for five minutes' time. You can only take a breath for now."

The breath provides a natural target to focus on. It grounds you in the here and now.

Seasoned meditators tell us that "the best time to awaken both the body and the spirit is in the early morning. We are fresh, in solitude, and the vibrations of the world are at their calmest. It is not surprising that you will find all experienced meditators and yogis up with the dawn. The first half hour of conscious awareness will be the foundation of your day. Make an early start. Meditate, set the switch of your consciousness and calibrate your energy for the day. You'll be surprised the difference it makes" (www.thoughtfortoday.org.uk).

There is a Zen story that describes the unquiet condition of the mind rather well. It is taken from the book *The Heart of the Buddha's Teaching* by Thich Nhat Hanh, a Zen master and teacher of mindfulness meditation. The story is about a man and a horse. The horse is galloping quickly, and it appears that the man on the horse is going somewhere important. Another man standing alongside the road shouts, "Where are you going?" and the first man replies, "I don't know! Ask the horse!"

This is also our story. We are riding a horse, we don't know where we are going, and we can't stop. The horse is our habit energy pulling us along. We are always running, and it has become a habit. We struggle all the time, even in our sleep. We are at war within ourselves, and we can easily start a war with others.

We say and do things we don't want to, causing suffering to others and ourselves, and afterward we regret these. We need to be mindful in order to stop this course of destruction. Mindfulness allows us to recognize our habits and prevent them from dominating us.

> Being unmindful is equivalent to not being here at all. We drink a cup of tea, but we are not aware that we are drinking a cup of tea. We sit with the person we love, but we don't know she is there. We are someplace else, thinking about the past or the future. Our habit energy is carrying us

along, and we are its captive. We need to shine the light of mindfulness on everything we do, and reclaim our liberty (Thich Naht Hanh).

An expert in body-mind medicine, Dr. Deepak Chopra strongly believes that meditation can benefit everyone. He tells us,

> Recent research shows meditation offers too many significant benefits to ignore. It refreshes us, helps us settle into what's happening now, helps us cope in a world that overloads us with information and communication, decreases over-thinking and worry, makes us more productive, and helps us sleep better.
>
> It is a myth to think that we have to be a certain way – more spiritual, more evolved, more peaceful, to successfully meditate - when meditation is what actually allows us to be all those things and more.

***

Many readers may be wondering what this *meditation* is all about and how we can do it. For anyone who has never tried to meditate and wants to, and for any beginner who thinks he is not doing it right, I will give the *simple method* that I use.

First of all, find a quiet place where you will not be disturbed. Sit cross-legged on a cushion on the floor, or sit on a chair with your feet resting on the floor. The important thing is to be comfortable.

Keep your back upright and straight without straining. Consciously relax your whole body. Become aware of your breathing without changing it in any way. Don't make it slower or quicker. Now focus on your in-breath and on your out-breath. You can say to yourself,

"Breathing in, I am aware that I am breathing in. Breathing out, I am aware that I am breathing out." Or just say, "In," for the inhale and, "Out," for the exhale.

By focusing on your body and your breath in this way, you are bringing mind and body together. Normally, our minds are scattered, rushing from thought to thought, worry to worry, memory to memory. Believe me, this restlessness of mind will continue as you try to meditate, but that's okay. Just bring your attention back to your breath. Again, become aware of the in-breath and the out-breath. When you feel discomfort in a part of your body, stay aware of the discomfort, and breathe with it. If you must, change your position and make yourself comfortable again.

Before you start, you may set a timer for five or more minutes. Choose a soft-sounding timer that will give you a gentle reminder of the time rather than a loud alarm that will jolt you out of your meditation.

There are many other meditation methods, some of which involve focusing on an object such as a flower or a candle flame. Using the breath is the easiest way since the breath is with us all the time wherever we go.

One can also do walking meditation. This is done by walking slowly and being aware of every step as each foot moves forward and touches the ground. This can be a pleasant way to meditate, and it can be done either before or after sitting meditation.

Bring a gentle awareness to all that occurs while you sit (or walk). Observe all that arises (e.g., discomfort) in your body and in your thoughts. Exercise unreactive awareness without judgment of whether it is good or bad. Bring your attention back to your breath.

Little by little, the mind learns to become calm and peaceful.

From this description, it is obvious that meditation is quite easy. What is difficult for most people is *finding time* to meditate. It is helpful to set time aside for it, making it an integral part of your schedule.

Nowadays the advice given to beginners is that it is not necessary to strictly follow a particular method but rather to find one's own way of relaxing and calming the mind. The secret to starting and sustaining a meditation practice is to find the simplest, most natural way to *stop* so that meditation will be *easy* to fit it into your busy life. The desired goal is to be in a relaxed state, physically and mentally. When our minds are clear of the endless chatter that normally resides there, we are able to deal more effectively with the challenges that come our way. It is in the stillness that the answers come, that we become receptive to wisdom and inspiration. Ideally, one learns to be present in the here and now all of the time.

Here are some words of wisdom from Ted Kunz's book *Peace Begins with Me*. "The solution is to *live in the present*. The present moment is always manageable. The future and past do not exist. They are illusions. To live in the present simply notice where you are. If you are in the future or the past, bring yourself into present moment awareness. A tool for doing this is to activate your senses—touch, listen, smell, taste, or consciously look at something—or become aware of your breathing." Kunz gives a simple exercise to achieve calmness and peace that I would like to share as it is similar to the meditation described previously, but it adds some focus on the body. I find this method helpful in bringing mind and body together at the beginning of meditation.

Take a few moments to fully become aware of the sensations in your right hand, and then focus on your left hand. Repeat with your right foot and left foot. Then after a while, shift your awareness to your breathing. Notice your breath moving in and out of your lungs, your chest expanding, your diaphragm moving.

Notice the peace and stillness within. The sense of calm and quiet may last a few minutes or even hours.

It is possible to access stillness and peacefulness any time you choose, especially when doing routine tasks. Use your senses to experience your present environment—smell, texture, sound, sight, and taste. Be aware of your breathing. By focusing your attention in the present, you gain the peacefulness of this moment.

I encountered the same approach in a wonderful book on mindfulness, one of the first that I read many years ago, specifically *Wherever You Go, There You Are*, which was written by Jon Kabat-Zinn. It is packed with guidance on how to stay present and mindful in all situations and to find joy in the simple things of life—even when doing mundane chores like washing dishes. Kabat-Zinn, professor emeritus at the University of Massachusetts Medical School, presents his ideas in a readable style that captures one's attention. I have read this book a number of times and believe that I have indeed internalized its message as I seem to be exceptionally mindful and aware of what is happening around me and within me. Kabat-Zinn created the Stress Reduction Clinic and the Center for Mindfulness, Health and Society at the previously mentioned university.

Today, meditation is acknowledged as a valuable tool in reducing stress and is increasingly used in the medical profession by psychotherapists and psychologists.

Mindfulness meditation has its roots in Buddhism, an ancient tradition with a psychological flavor that originated in India. Its founder, the Buddha, was not interested in satisfying human curiosity about the nature of the divine or similar questions. He was concerned exclusively with the human situation and the suffering of human beings (see chapter 10, "The Ancient Wisdom of the East").

My own experience with meditation developed when I discovered the Mindfulness Community of Israel, which comprises a group of wonderful people who follow and strive to live up to the teachings of Thich Nhat Hanh, a Vietnamese monk and one of the most respected and recognized Zen masters in the world.

Thich Nhat Hanh is a man of great wisdom, a teacher, and the author of more than thirty books that have been translated into many languages. In his youth he was exiled from his homeland for being a peace activist and has lived abroad ever since. He has founded monasteries and spiritual centers in the United States, France, Germany, and other countries. He now lives and teaches in the spiritual center he founded in France called Plum Village, and he has a large following across the world.

***

A slightly different take on meditation is given by Joey Korn, author of *Dowsing: A Path to Enlightenment*. Korn writes, "Meditation is a place you enter, not a thing you do. It is a place of stillness. A place of Light where all inspired thought comes from. The many meditative techniques are avenues upon which you can travel to reach this inner place."

I found Joey Korn, a spiritual dowser, by chance. His website (www. dowsers.com) captivated me. I bought his book (mentioned above) and attended one of his workshops. Thanks to him, I learned about a great man named Walter Russell (1871–1963), whom Korn mentions in both his website and his book. Russell's impressive achievements are described in chapter 12, "Spiritual Connection."

Walter Russell considered meditation to have a spiritual function for mankind, and thought it was extremely important for people who are enslaved by the demands of physical things and are unable to hear the voice within. "It transports you from the material world of the senses to the world of the soul." For him, meditation was a time to communicate with God and to be at one with Him.

The only journey worth taking is the journey within.

—William Yeats, poet

Chapter 10

The Ancient Wisdom of the East

Buddhism is an ancient tradition dating back to the sixth century BC. It is not a religion. It follows the teachings of the founder of this tradition, the Buddha. (The word Buddha means the "awakened" or "enlightened" one.) He is not worshipped as a god, and Buddhists do not pray to him. He is their teacher. Neither do they relate to the existence of a supernatural power to be obeyed and feared, a power that rewards and punishes and controls our destiny. "Buddhism expounds no dogmas that one must blindly believe, no creeds that one must accept on good faith without reasoning, no superstitious rites and ceremonies to be observed for formal entry into the fold, no meaningless sacrifices and penances for one's purification" (Narada, 1964).

Buddhism centers on understanding the self and strives to reduce suffering. Instead of prayers, the Buddha emphasizes the importance of meditation that promotes self-discipline, self-purification, and enlightenment. It serves as a tonic both to the mind and the heart (Narada).

Since I am not an expert on Buddhism, the best I can do is to present its basic principles and let you judge the nature of this path for yourself—but first, a few words about its founder, Gautama Buddha.

The historical Buddha's name was Siddhartha Gautama. He was born circa 500 BC at Kapilavatthu on the Indian border of present-day Nepal. He was born to a royal family and raised as a prince. He lived a pampered life, and in order to be protected from the realities of the world outside, he was restricted to the palace and its immediate surroundings. Gautama must have received a good education, but no details are known about it. Since he belonged to a warrior race, he received special training in the art of warfare. At age sixteen he married his beautiful cousin, who bore him a child. He was curious about the world outside and eventually slipped out to see it for himself. He was shocked to see so much suffering in the form of poverty, infirmity, illness, and death. He sought to understand that world, and after much thought he decided to leave his closeted life.

"The allurements of the palace were no longer cherished objects of delight to him. The time was right to depart. At the age of 29 he renounced the plentitude of wealth and prosperity and began his historic journey. He became a penniless wanderer, living on charity. With no possessions but a bowl to collect food, he went on the quest of Truth and Peace" (Narada).

Gautama found distinguished teachers with whom he stayed so that he could learn from them. He gained complete mastery of his mind, but his ultimate goal was not achieved, namely his quest for the complete cessation of suffering. He realized that there was no one capable enough to teach him what he yearned for—the highest truth. He spent time alone meditating and came to the realization that the highest truth is to be found within oneself.

After his enlightenment he began to teach his doctrine to others. He formulated the **Four Noble Truths**, which are the foundations of his teachings.

1. All life is suffering.

2. The cause of suffering is attachment (to people, things, or situations).

3. Suffering can be ended.

4. The Eightfold Path is the only straight way to liberation and the end of suffering (Nirvana).

The Four Noble Truths are well explained by the authors Capra and Thich Nhat Hanh among others.

1. The First Noble Truth states the outstanding characteristic of the human situation, which is *suffering*. This comes from our difficulty in facing the basic fact of life, that everything around us is impermanent and transitory. The notion that change is the basic feature of nature lies at the root of Buddhism.

2. The Second Noble Truth deals with the *cause* of all suffering, which in the Buddhist view, arises whenever we resist the flow of life and try to cling to people, things, events, or ideas. We cling to things that we see as firm and persistent but in fact are transient and ever-changing.

3. The Third Noble Truth states that the *cessation of suffering* is possible through nonattachment and that total liberation (Nirvana), the ultimate goal of Buddhism, can be achieved by the eradication of all forms of craving.

4. The Fourth Noble Truth is the Buddha's prescription to end all suffering, the Eightfold Path of self-development.

The Buddha regarded his doctrine as a means to achieve enlightenment. His focus was on the *impermanence* of all things. He insisted on freedom from spiritual authority (including his own), saying that he could only show the *way* to enlightenment and that it was up to every individual to tread his way to the end through his or her own efforts.

A Bit of Humor:

A student went to his meditation teacher and said, "My
meditation is horrible! My legs ache, or I'm constantly
falling asleep. I feel so distracted. It's just horrible!"
"It will pass," the teacher said matter-of-factly.
A week later the student came back to his
teacher. "My meditation is wonderful!
I feel so aware, so peaceful, so alive! It's just wonderful!"
"It will pass," the teacher replied matter-of-factly.

The Eightfold Path

1. **Right View or Understanding**: This is the realization that
   the way we live, our state of mind, and all our actions have
   consequences. We cannot lay the burden on someone else
   or on some deity. When we suffer (because of fear, loss,
   jealousy, hatred, and anger), the right view or understanding
   will show us that this is not due to our surroundings or other
   people. It is our own creation because of our mental state.
2. **Right Thought**: Wishing to free the mind from the negative
   forces within us—hatred, anger, selfishness, and the obsessive
   desire for sensual experience. These forces lead to hurtfulness
   in our relationship with others and even in ourselves.
3. **Right Speech**: Using speech that is kind and promotes
   harmony, avoid malicious gossip as well as abusive and harsh
   speech, and be honest.
4. **Right Action**: Respecting the feelings of others, respecting
   their property, understanding our sexual nature, refraining
   from all forms of sexual misconduct. In order to have this
   control over our body and speech, it is essential to be in
   control of our mental faculties. Therefore, we choose to
   avoid alcohol and drugs that cause heedlessness and impede
   our alertness and our ability to train ourselves.

5. **Right Livelihood**: We must train ourselves to earn our living without exploiting or hurting others—people and animals.

6. **Right Effort**: Making an effort to train our minds to abandon that which is harmful and to develop that which is skillful.

7. **Right Mindfulness**: Being aware of the present moment, of what we are doing, saying, and thinking. Taking responsibility for cultivating this quality of being awake. We must make this a part of our daily lives. Without mindfulness, there is no training. There is only habitual, mechanical, instinctual behavior.

8. **Right Concentration**: Being able to focus our attention on the present moment and looking deeply into the nature of our feelings, emotions, and thoughts, the nature of the mind itself.

The Eightfold Path is a wonderful tool by which to live the Buddhist's way of life. The steps are interrelated and interdependent. You can see the path unfolding. As our thoughts and aspirations become purer, our speech and actions, the way we live, and the mind itself will become more refined, more caring and peaceful. Strengthening one aspect helps to strengthen the other factors on the path and reach the right awareness of reality.

It is very obvious to me that anyone who sincerely adopts the principles of Buddhism and tries to live by them is on the path to *right living*. The wisdom in this ancient tradition is relevant to our lives today, maybe more so than ever, considering the hectic pace and countless distractions that keep us outwardly focused and rob us of the tranquility we need to maintain a healthy mind.

I would like to illustrate how embracing this wisdom can help us in our everyday lives by describing the Buddhist teaching called the

Three Poisons (greed, hatred, and delusion) followed by a real-life example involving a friend of mine.

The Three Poisons cause us confusion, unhappiness, and suffering. Understanding them empowers us to gain clarity and insight, enabling us to eliminate them and find inner peace. It follows from the teaching of the Four Noble Truths (see previous) that when we accept and understand the causes of our suffering, we can take the necessary steps to remove them and liberate ourselves.

Greed: Greed prevents us from showing generosity and compassion toward others and also manifests itself in the way we treat the environment and behave in the world of business. It is an endless cycle that brings only suffering and unhappiness. We want the objects of our desire to provide us with lasting satisfaction so we feel fulfilled; however, once we attain what we want, our greed and desire arises, and we look outside of ourselves for the next thing that will hopefully bring satisfaction. We are never content.

Hatred: Hatred can show up as anger, hostility, aversion, or ill will to another person. Hatred or anger thrusts us into a vicious cycle of always finding conflict and enemies around us, making our mind neurotic. We are endlessly occupied with strategies of self-protection or revenge. With the poison of hatred, we create conflict and enemies in the world around us and within our own being.

Delusion: Delusion feeds our misperception or wrong understanding of reality. Delusion is our inability to understand the nature of things exactly as they are. The result is that we are not in harmony with ourselves, others, or life.

I first became aware of this teaching of the Three Poisons when a friend who has been practicing mindfulness meditation for many years described how she found herself engaging all three poisons that very day at the supermarket!

It started with the purchase of a large number of items that were on sale at a reduced price. My friend—whom I will call Rose—didn't need to buy so much food that day, but she bought it because of the low price, thinking she was saving money (greed). Then at the checkout counter, the clerk spoke to her rudely. Rose took offense and reacted aggressively, lashing out at the girl (hatred). Finally, when she was home, she realized that her refrigerator was now packed with stuff she couldn't use and would eventually have to throw out (delusion). Clearly, she didn't feel happy after her visit to the supermarket. Neither the dent in her wallet nor the state of her refrigerator brought her any joy. Regarding the clerk at the checkout point, Rose reckoned that the girl was probably exhausted after hours of dealing with people and needed compassion rather than sharp words.

The understanding that Rose gained from her behavior in terms of her Buddhist training was an eye-opener to her.

Transforming the Three Poisons

The Buddha taught us that the poisons of greed, hatred, and delusion can be purified and transformed. The work requires patience, persistence, and deep compassion for ourselves and others. The goal is to liberate ourselves from the acquired habits that obscure clarity and rob us of joy.

This work of purification must take place in the precise place where the poisons originate, namely in the mind itself, when they first appear. It requires calming the mind and seeing deeply into ourselves. Being mindful and aware, we can then discern how these deep-seated poisons influence our everyday thoughts, feelings, speech, and actions. This leads to understanding, which is the beginning of our ability to transform these poisons. To accomplish this awareness, we train our mind through meditation, which helps us to become more aware of ourselves in everyday situations. Then we are able to notice when thoughts and emotions arise and begin to disturb us. In this way we can work with them before they get out of control, causing harm to ourselves and others. More about this teaching can be found at https://mettarefuge.wordpress.com/2010/06/16/transforming-the-three-poisons-greed-hatred-and-delusion/ and www.naljorprisondharmaservice.org/pdf/ThreePoisons.htm.

Our practice of mindfulness keeps us in a state of awareness that helps us cope with different challenges. For example, during a heated conversation with your partner or your children, becoming aware that misunderstanding and hostility are escalating, you can request a break so that each side can cool down. Again, I give a real-life example that I learned from my friend Rose (mentioned previously). During a heated argument with her son, Rose mindfully examined the behavior taking place and the feelings that were being aroused. She requested that they take a short break from the argument. Afterward, the discussion continued, but in a completely different tone. A major clash was avoided, and with skill, a potentially explosive exchange ended on a friendly tone with a hug and words of appreciation.

I have witnessed examples of people behaving in this way, demonstrating how mindfulness can change lives for the better. It involves first becoming aware of what is happening in the moment. Is there discomfort? First, calm the mind, look within, and examine the cause of the discomfort or suffering. The next step is to decide how to remove the cause of the suffering, and then mindfully engage in *right action* with compassion and pure intent.

"Only when we find the quietness in our minds can we begin to hear our inner teacher, so that we may receive some in-tuition. Only when we are ready to recognize and value the wisdom that we carry at the core of our being will we turn our attention inward and 'listen in'. A little practice and patience will be needed. Sit down, be quiet and listen and you might be surprised at what you hear. Then do it again tomorrow.

All you need to do is remember that you are the listener and not the noise"

—Thought for Today at info@thoughtfortoday.org.uk).

***

There is one last gem that I want to impart, which for me is the cherry on the top of my experience with Buddhism. It is a basic code of ethics known as the Five Precepts. It is also known as the Five Mindfulness Trainings in some Buddhist practices. The Buddhist tradition acknowledges that life is complex and filled with many difficulties, and rather than speaking of actions being right or wrong, Buddhism speaks of living skillfully or unskillfully. These teachings are an inspiration to people who strive to achieve the Buddhist ideals and way of life.

Here is a condensed version of the Five Mindfulness Trainings.

1. **Reverence for Life.** Aware of the suffering caused by the destruction of life, I am committed to cultivating compassion and to protecting the lives of people, animals, plants, and

the earth. I am determined not to kill, not to let others kill, and not to support any act of killing in the world.

2. **True Happiness.** Aware of the suffering caused by exploitation, social injustice, and oppression, I am committed to practicing generosity in my thinking, speaking, and acting. I am determined not to steal and not to possess anything that should belong to others. I will share my time, energy, and material resources with those who are in need. I am aware I can live happily as I already have more than enough conditions to be happy.

3. **True Love.** Aware of the suffering caused by sexual misconduct, I am committed to cultivating responsibility and learning ways to protect the safety and integrity of individuals, couples, families, and society. I am determined not to engage in sexual relations without love and a long-term commitment made known to my family and friends. I will do everything in my power to protect children from sexual abuse and to prevent couples and families from being broken by sexual misconduct.

4. **Loving Speech and Deep Listening.** Aware of the suffering caused by unmindful speech and the inability to listen to others, I am committed to cultivating loving speech and compassionate listening in order to relieve suffering and to promote reconciliation and peace in myself and among other people. Knowing that words can create happiness or suffering, I am committed to speaking truthfully, using words that inspire confidence, joy, and hope. I am determined not to utter words that can cause division or discord.

5. **Nourishment and Healing.** Aware of the suffering caused by unmindful consumption, I am committed to cultivating good health, both physical and mental, by mindful eating, drinking, and consuming. I am determined not to use alcohol or drugs, or any products that contain toxins, such

as certain websites, TV programs, films, magazines, books, and conversations.

***

The Buddhist Guidelines for Right Living

- Awareness of *suffering*, its causes, and ways to reduce/eliminate it
- Accepting the *impermanence* of all things
- The belief that we are *all connected*, all one
- Striving always to be *compassionate* to all beings
- Aiming to *understand the workings of the mind*, to be constantly aware of our thoughts, feelings, and actions, and thus mindful of our interactions with others

Such mindfulness is cultivated through meditation, the essence of Buddhism.

My religion is very simple. My religion is kindness.

—The Dalai Lama

There is much more to Buddhism than what is described here. I have given only an introduction for the benefit of readers who are new to the subject.

The Buddhist doctrine is homocentric, teaching that *we ourselves* are responsible for our behavior and its consequences, as opposed to the doctrines of theocentric religions, which rely on an outside force. It teaches how to understand our minds and train them through awareness and meditation. It originated with the Buddha, the enlightened one, who passed on his wisdom about a way of life that honors all humans, animals, and the earth.

Following the Buddhist teachings does not require that you change your religious beliefs, or traditions, only that you strive to be the best person possible.

In my opinion, it doesn't get any better than this.

***

I have described the *mental* aspects of well-being as taught by Eastern traditions, but there is a physical part as well, provided by *yoga*. The practice of yoga can be divided into hatha yoga, which focuses on the breath and discipline of the body through physical exercises or postures, and raja-yoga, which is concerned with discipline of the mind through concentration and meditation. Yoga also includes specific dietary recommendations that are deemed beneficial to our physical and emotional health. The yoga diet is vegetarian and avoids stimulants such as coffee and alcohol (Hawskley and Whitelaw, 1995).

Yoga connects the movement of the body to the breath and to the mind. Connecting body, mind, and breath helps us to direct our attention inward to cultivate an awareness of the body and the mind's thought patterns. The yoga philosophy of mastery over the body and understanding the mind originated in India an estimated four thousand years ago. "Yoga works. Nothing which did not work could survive for three to four thousand years. It works because it is continually evolving. Although its ultimate concern is with human development at the highest levels, its continual evolution makes it unlike religions, which tend to become fossilized around the sayings of their founders" (Hutchinson).

In his book *The Spirit of Healing*, physician David Cumes writes about the benefits of yoga as follows: "Moving meditations such as yoga and tai chi that direct us inward are more powerful than regular exercise. This is the reason hatha yoga has become so popular in the West. Although the postures, or *asanas*, are only a small part of yoga philosophy – the healing consequences of this form of stretching and breathing can have a miraculous effect, not only on the body but on the psyche as well."

Yoga may interweave other philosophies such as Hinduism or Buddhism, but it is not necessary to study those paths or to abandon your own religious beliefs in order to practice yoga (Hutchinson).

The primary principle of yoga is *non-harm* to self and others. This includes all animals, hence the strict vegetarian diet.

Recently, I attended a weekend yoga retreat and experienced firsthand the amazing teachings of one of the most ancient texts of the East, the Bhagavada Gita. This seven-hundred-verse Hindu scripture in Sanskrit from around the third millennium BC is packed with wisdom that relates to everyday life. I am always amazed by the profound wisdom found in foreign ancient texts such as this one. It matches the best of our Western teachings.

I have been practicing hatha yoga for many years and can feel that it enhances my physical well-being. I recommend it as a form of exercise that is highly beneficial and can be practiced by everyone, young and old.

Namaste

Holding the hands together palm-to-palm, usually accompanied with a light bow and the word *Namaste* is a form of salutation throughout Asia. The word Namaste is derived from Sanskrit and means "I bow to the divinity within you from the divinity within me." In yoga this posture is always held at chest (heart) level and touching the body. It elicits a state of calmness and inner peace. In some Buddhist circles, the palms may be held slightly apart (cupped) in this position, symbolizing a lotus flower bud. Lotus plants grow in mud with their stems reaching up through the water. The flowers, which are clean and free of mud, rise up into the sunlight. The symbolism of this is that man can rise from the mud of materialism into the sunshine of enlightenment.

The palm-to-palm posture is also used in other parts of the world, and its meaning varies depending on the culture. In the West, it is referred to as the prayer position. It may symbolize veneration of a higher power, supplication, sincerity, repentance, or obedience.

I have discovered something about the prayer position that I find interesting. I have not read or heard about this before, and I give my interpretation here:

As described in chapter 5, we have a number of energy centers or chakras in our bodies, the seven main ones being located along the vertebral column. There are other energy centers in the body, such as the hands and feet. The rotating energy of the chakra can be detected by holding a pendulum above it. The pendulum rotates in the same direction as the chakra. Regarding the hands, one can observe the pendulum rotating clockwise for the right palm and fingertips and counterclockwise for the left palm and fingertips.

When the hands are held together in the prayer position, the energies in both hands (and all the fingertips) rotate in the same direction. *My interpretation of this is that when the vital energy from the two sides of the body moves in unison, there is an enhancement of overall energy.* Furthermore, bringing the hands together at the center of the body *connects the left and right sides of the body as well as the left and right hemispheres of the brain.* The latter is significant in integrating full brain function as occurs in the brain gym exercises described by Dennison (2006) and Hannaford (2005).

It would be interesting to know how this hand gesture originated. There is a theory that suggests it comes from the position of prisoners' hands when tied together and that it symbolizes submission and obedience. However, this posture has been found in archeological clay figures and seals dating to earlier than 3000 BC, suggesting a less hostile origin.

The praying hands posture is known to have a long history in Judaism and Christianity. It may be more significant and beneficial than we are aware of. I suspect the ancients knew something that we are completely unaware of.

Part 3

Spiritual Well-being

Introduction to Spiritual Well-being

A healthy body and a clear mind are magnificent assets that enable us to live a good life. However, ask someone who *has it all* if he feels happy and fulfilled, and in most cases, he will answer, "Yes, but something is missing."

Because the human being is *more* than a biological machine powered by thousands of biochemical reactions, purely material supplies and services are not enough to feed the entire being. Many of us experience a spiritual hunger that no material success can feed.

Only through awareness of the body-mind-spirit connection and full participation of all three can we live full and balanced lives.

Our bodies are physical expressions of Spirit.

—Rabbi Michael Laitman, philosopher and kabbalist

Part 3 of this book focuses on our connection with our own spiritual self and with the world of spirit that exists beyond our three-dimensional level of existence.

Chapter 11

Religion

If the only prayer you ever say in your entire life is
"Thank You,"
It will be enough.

—Meister Eckhart, philosopher and
theologian (thirteenth century)

We are all part of some religion or belief system either by birth or by choice. Some people identify very strongly with their religious affiliation, others less so. For some people, their religion represents *who* they are. All this is normal and acceptable, and I have no argument with it.

Many people, however, recoil from the concept of God. I know people who feel part of a certain religious tradition yet find it difficult to *believe*, and strongly deny the existence of God.

There is something about the way religion is taught that turns many people away. It smacks of dogma, illogical rules, and punishment. Other negative concepts include the pervading belief that God controls us with an iron fist, is quick to anger, and takes revenge on us for our weaknesses. Some religions teach that the ordinary, mundane pleasures of life are sinful, causing an unnecessary clash between our natural drives and God's "expectations" of us. Most religions control people through fear, namely the fear of being doomed to eternal damnation (in the fires of hell, according to some). It's no wonder that so many people grow up with feelings of guilt, failure, and unworthiness. All of this provides the perfect breeding ground for nonbelievers and the feeling that religion and any hint of spirituality are irrelevant in our lives.

We have assigned certain human attributes to God. We humanize Him as being angry, jealous, and revengeful. How small we have made the Creator of the universe. Thankfully, we also honor Him with the qualities of forgiveness, compassion, and generosity— otherwise life would be a real hell!

We grow up with the notion that God is in control of our lives and everything that happens in the world, so when things go wrong, we accept it as God's will. People blame God for allowing wars to happen, forgetting that *men* start wars, not God. There is no evidence that anyone other than Man starts wars and carries out atrocities against other humans. In the course of our history and even today, wars and brutality are executed in the name of God for His glory and to protect His teachings! How absurd.

I personally consider myself to be deeply religious, meaning that I believe in a benevolent supreme being or creative source, which I equate with the concept of God or Spirit. I had the good fortune to be raised by parents who believed. I am convinced that growing up with a religious background is an advantage. If the beliefs that one grows up with do not suit us when we are older, we can discard them. But if we do not learn about these things at a young age, how can we make informed choices when we are older?

My parents were moderately religious, and from a young age, much of my life was in some way connected with how God wants us to behave. I was fortunate that my parents were sincere in their beliefs and tried to live up to the teachings of their faith, so I was not exposed to the hypocrisy that turns so many people against religion. My father especially was what I would call a true believer who was close to his God in daily life. He prayed a lot, and now I realize how *connected* he was as I recall that whenever an ambulance sped past with its siren sounding, he would pray silently for the unfortunate person inside. To me, that is being religious in the best sense of the word, especially because my father didn't care if the person in the ambulance was white, black, Christian, Jewish, or Muslim. He also didn't care much about religious authorities and their rules. My mother took religious dogma more seriously and followed her religion more by the book.

Although my parents thought that their own faith was the true one, they had nothing against other religions, since all religions worship the same God. This was wonderful to grow up with as I learned to accept others for who they are without being influenced by the religion they belong to.

I believe that at its core, every religion provides sound guiding principles for humanity. Our divinely inspired scriptures comprise elevated values that empower us to live wisely with our fellow man. *So why is the world in such a mess?* Apart from the fact that society is made up of humans with their greed for power, our religious institutions are also run by imperfect humans with their own greed for power. Many religions control our thoughts and behavior, mostly through fear of God, keeping us subservient and ignorant of our own ability to connect with the Creator without intermediaries. For centuries this control by religious authorities has robbed people of their birthright to live self-empowered lives. In the dark ages, freethinkers were excommunicated by the church or worse, burned at the stake. The same fate awaited healers (witches), adherents of other religions, and any dissident who did not toe the religious line. These people presented a threat to the authority of the church and its control over people's minds. We have come a long way since those hellish days.

***

We are the creators of our own destinies. We need to break free of the antiquated concept that we are helpless and at the mercy of the big guy in the sky who punishes us if we don't adhere to all the man-made laws that religion has imposed on us. In religious prayers we refer to God as our Father. Assuming that we are indeed created by Him, then this is a fitting title. Can you imagine saying to your child, "You are going to be tested every day of your life. If you dare step out of line, I will punish you." No, you tell your child, "I will always be here for you to protect and help you." When he falls, you pick him up and comfort him. That is the God I believe in.

The majority of the world's population is monotheistic, yet there are thousands of different rules, man's rules. Which of them are right? Does it really matter if your friend/neighbor believes he has to dress in a certain way or face a certain direction when he prays? What is important is that he connects to the divine with pure intent. Let others honor God in their own way. If it brings them inner peace, that is what counts.

In this new age, people are rejecting the incongruities of organized religion and are seeking that which nourishes the soul. In my experience, the ritual and ceremony does not provide much soul food, although I acknowledge that for many people being part of a religious community gives them a feeling of belonging. The emotional comfort of socializing with people of like mind (regardless of their depth of belief) has its value. Yes, one's place of worship should be a sacred space for connecting with God and with people.

I recently came across a book titled *Who Needs God* written by Rabbi Harold Kushner, in which he discusses organized religion in a convincingly positive way. "It offers us a place to which we can bring our whole selves, not just that part of ourselves that we bring to our jobs and our hobbies, and to encounter the whole selves of our neighbors in a way we cannot meet them anywhere else." Kushner says that organized religion can offer us a vision of a world where people no longer condemn themselves to loneliness by seeing all other people as rivals. "Religion is not primarily a set of beliefs, a collection of prayers, or a series of rituals. Religion is first and foremost a way of seeing. It can't change the facts about the world we live in, but it can change the way we see those facts, and that in itself can often make a real difference."

Kushner shows how religious commitment can have a place in our lives, filling a need for belonging on a social level as well as the need for spiritual connection. He does not insist that his religion is the only one that teaches the right way to live. For the lucky ones, their religion does indeed provide a safe haven, especially if it is managed by someone like the previously mentioned author—a sound model who is open-minded and wise and acknowledges the brotherhood of man rather than focusing on the differences between people. A person who is truly connected.

Kushner has written the best seller *When Bad Things Happen to Good People,* and other books, namely, *Living a Life that Matters, The Lord Is My Shepherd: Healing Wisdom of the Twenty-Third Psalm, When All You've Ever Wanted Isn't Enough,* and *To Life!* I haven't read these books, but I mention them because I am impressed with Kushner's philosophy of life and his sincere approach to religion. They may be of benefit to anyone who is searching for meaning, connection, or inspiration.

My views on religion are colored by my own experience of it being devoid of spirituality. I reject the tactics that some institutions use to control people's lives by posing as the only source of knowledge about God and the only route to God Himself. They teach about a distant authoritarian God who is in total control of our lives and demands obedience through fear. Much human bias has been added to the divinely inspired teachings that were recorded centuries ago. Much of this bias and its man-made laws might have served a purpose in times gone by but are now outdated and meaningless to many. I do not mean to detract from the traditional ways of worship; however, the world has changed, and today people need more. Some religious authorities fabricate rules that minimize and disempower the individual instead of teaching about the greatness of connecting directly with the Creator. There are many ways to connect with Spirit, and each person has his own path. Today more than ever before, we are free to choose how to connect with our Creator/Spirit/ God in whichever way suits us best.

All men have access to God but each man has a different access.
—Martin Buber, philosopher

In the final analysis, what truly matters is that one's religion nourishes the soul and is uplifting. If instead it makes you feel disempowered, then that particular stream of religion does not fulfill its role. Alternatively, the religious principles may be sound, but the leader(s) may be misinformed or dysfunctional. Anyone who finds himself in such a situation should drop that particular stream or place of worship for one that is empowering and spiritually uplifting.

***

A Bit of Humor:

Who was Jesus?

There are three good arguments that Jesus was black.

1. He called everyone brother.
2. He liked gospel.
3. He couldn't get a fair trial.

But then there are three equally good arguments that Jesus was Jewish.

1. He went into His Father's business.
2. He lived at home until He was thirty-three.
3. He was sure His mother was a virgin, and His mother was sure He was God.

But then there are three equally good arguments that Jesus was Italian.

1. He talked with His hands.
2. He had wine with His meals.
3. He used olive oil.

But then there are three equally good arguments that Jesus was a Californian.

1. He wore long hair.
2. He walked around barefoot.
3. He started a new religion.

But then there are three equally good arguments that Jesus was a Native American.

1. He was at peace with nature.

2. He ate a lot of fish.
3. He talked about the Great Spirit.

But then there are three equally good arguments that Jesus was Irish.

1. He never got married.
2. He was always telling stories.
3. He loved green pastures.

But the most compelling evidence of all, three proofs that Jesus was a woman.

1. He fed a crowd at a moment's notice when there was no food.
2. He tried to get a message across to a bunch of men who just didn't get it.
3. And even when He was dead, He had to get up because there was work to do.

—Author unknown

Prayer

One often hears the statement that "prayer is talking to God while meditation is listening to Him." We also hear people complain that their prayers are not answered.

Prayer has been with us for centuries, and there are different ways to pray. In the long-established religions, the traditional prayers consist of reading endless pages of repetitive praise of God's greatness, and supplication for help. From personal experience this kind of prayer loses its value because it is repetitive and boring, and even though the eyes continue to read the words, the mind wanders—sometimes in undesirable directions! This was the kind of praying that I grew up with, and I was astonished to witness a different kind of prayer I encountered by chance at the meetings of other more dynamic traditions. Here people spoke to God as you would speak to someone you know and respect. I was impressed.

Of course, in all religious traditions, there are set prayers that are usually recited aloud by the congregation. These are traditional prayers that have been used for centuries and have a unifying effect as they carry a deep meaning. They are also relatively short (e.g., the Christian "Our Father" and the Jewish "Shema Israel").

Everyone who *believes* prays, and in times of crisis, even those who do not believe pray. It is intuitive. The intellect may tell us otherwise, but the soul knows.

I consider prayer to be profound communication with our source. A true connection is uplifting, and one feels it internally. This kind of praying is focused and done with intention.

Dawson Church cites studies that provide evidence that prayer has a definite beneficial effect on people suffering from various ailments. "Prayer is one of the most powerful forms in which intention may be packaged. Prayer has been the subject of hundreds of studies, most of which have demonstrated that patients who are prayed for get better faster." More than a thousand scientific studies have demonstrated that prayer, intention, and distant healing significantly affect health and longevity. These are reported in medical journals such as the *Annals of Internal Medicine* and the *Journal of Alternative and Complementary Medicine.*

Gregg Braden, a geologist and computer scientist, is a pioneer in bridging science, spirituality, and the real world. He, too, believes in the power of prayer, but he fully understood how prayer works only after studying the ancient wisdom in the Dead Sea Scrolls.

The entire Isaiah scroll was the only manuscript that was found intact among the Dead Sea Scrolls in 1946. Braden read the new translations of the original Aramaic manuscript and discovered the lost mode of prayer. In his book *The Isaiah Effect*, he tells us that 500 BC, the Essenes knew how to focus the power of prayer. They wrote that thought, feeling, and emotion are required for effective prayer. "The secret of prayer transcends the words of praise, the incantations and rhythmic chants, and abides in the feelings that the words evoke in us. The feeling can only exist when there is thought and emotion, as it represents the union of the two. When we feel, we are experiencing the desire of our emotion fused with the imagination of our thoughts. The feeling is the key to prayer."

All three (thinking, feeling, and emotion) must be aligned, meaning they must work together in union to focus the energy. This mode of prayer invites us to clearly and powerfully *feel* as if our prayers have already been answered (Braden).

Braden accepts the ancient text as a teaching that is relevant for us today.

> First shall the Son of Man seek peace within his own body; for his body is as a mountain pond that reflects the sun when it is still and clear. When it is full of mud and stones it reflects nothing. Then shall the Son of Man seek peace within his own thoughts … there is no greater power in heaven and earth than the thought of the Son of Man. Though unseen by the eyes of the body, yet each thought has mighty strength, even such strength can shake the heavens. Then shall the Son of Man seek peace with his own feelings. We call on the Angel of love to enter our feelings, that they may be purified. And all that was before impatience and discord will turn into harmony and peace. (Essene Gospel of Peace, book 4)

The power of *belief* is an integral part of effective prayer. In the gospel of John (16:23–24), we are told to believe that what we ask for will be given.

Author and visionary Neville Goddard, author of the *Power of Awareness*, proposed the idea of unifying thought, emotion, and feeling and assuming that our prayer has already happened. "You must abandon yourself mentally to your wish fulfilled in your love for that state, and in so doing, live in the new state and no more from the old state." Goddard's writings are based on what he called "the Law," the technique of creating one's physical reality through imagining. He tells us to make our dream a present fact by assuming the *feeling* of our wish fulfilled.

This is a modern take on the words of Jesus as stated in Matthew 21:22, "You can get anything—*anything* you ask for in prayer—if you believe it." (The Living Bible Paraphrased, USA ed.)

Support from eternal energy is available, but not always called upon in the appropriate manner.

—Veronica as channeled by the medium April Crawford

Chapter 12

Spiritual Connection

It is important to distinguish religion from spirituality,
since while they may overlap it's entirely possible to be
spiritual without being religious and vice versa.

—Joan Borysenko, psychologist and researcher (medical sciences)

Dr. Eric Pearl, author of *The Reconnection*, writes, "I used to think that people fell into one of three groups: those who don't believe in anything beyond their basic five senses, those who are open to the possibility that there might be something beyond those senses, and those who definitely believe there is something more. Yet suddenly I find myself in a fourth smaller group: those who *know* there's something more."

Lasting joy is what we are all striving for. We try to find it in places, events, people, love, and books. Why is it that most of us have not found it? Could it be we are looking in the wrong places? Searching for it *out there* when perhaps we would find it right here. And I don't mean *here* in this place, but closer even, within ourselves. More and more people are turning inward in their quest for real, lasting happiness. When we are in touch with our inner being, we connect to an integral part of the world of spirit.

The human condition has been described as "the heartbreaking inability to sustain contentment" by author Elizabeth Gilbert. Buddhism says that the human mind in its normal state *generates* suffering or misery. Hinduism sees this dysfunction as a form of collective mental illness. Taoists call it imbalance.

Eckhart Tolle (author of the best seller *The Power of Now*) states in his book *A New Earth* that the *normal* state of mind of most human beings contains a strong element of what we might call dysfunction or even madness. Different schools of thought over the centuries have found different explanations for Man's apparently inherent flawed state. The Christian tradition attributes all our suffering to original sin. But Tolle points out that the word *sin* has been greatly misunderstood and misinterpreted. Translated from the ancient Greek in which the New Testament was written, to sin means to miss the mark, to *miss the point* of human existence. It means to live unskillfully, blindly, and thus to suffer and cause suffering.

Other traditions use different terms to explain the human condition. Yogis believe that human discontentment is a simple case of mistaken identity. We're miserable because we wrongly believe that our limited little egos constitute our whole entire nature. We have failed to recognize our *divine* character. We don't realize that somewhere within us all, there exists a supreme self who is our true identity and is eternally at peace. Before you realize this truth, say the yogis, you will always be in despair (Gilbert).

You bear God within you, poor wretch, and know it not.

—Epictetus, Greek philosopher

We search for happiness everywhere, but we are like Tolstoy's beggar who spent his life sitting on a pot of gold, begging for pennies from every passerby, unaware that his fortune was right under him the whole time. Or consider the young hero of Paulo Coelho's *The Alchemist*, who traveled across the Mediterranean and northern Africa to the pyramids in search of a treasure only to find it finally in the most unexpected place of all.

Neurologist Dr. Eben Alexander had always believed that consciousness, thought, emotions, and spirit were simply productions of the brain (matter). However, after experiencing a near-death experience (described below), he now understands just how blind to the full nature of the spiritual universe we are on earth. "For all the successes of Western civilization, the world has paid a dear price in terms of the most crucial component of existence—our human spirit. Our focus on exponential progress in science and technology has left many of us bereft in the realm of meaning and joy, and of knowing how our lives fit into the grand scheme of existence for all eternity."

We tend to respect and even worship the rational aspect of our being and to dismiss or deny our ***intuition***. In his book *Mind Power into the 21st Century*, John Kehoe writes, "Our rational mind is like a computer—it processes the input it receives and calculates logical conclusions based on this information. But the rational mind is finite; it can only compute with the input it has received directly. The intuitive mind, on the other hand, seems to have access to an infinite supply of information. It appears to be able to tap into a deep storehouse of knowledge and wisdom, the universal mind." He cites numerous successful people who admit to relying on their intuition, among them billionaire Ted Turner, founder of CNN and Ray Kroc, who started McDonald's.

Many of the most successful people we know of have attributed their success in business, science, or the arts to being able to *plug into* their *intuition*. *The Harvard Business Review* reported a study conducted on high-ranking executives and found that they relied on hunches to cope with problems that were too complex for rational thinking. The study concluded that success does not lie in that narrow-minded concept called *rationality*. Success requires a blend of clear-headed logic and powerful intuition.

"Socrates said he was guided by his inner voice. Einstein, Edison, Marconi, Henry Ford, Luther Burbank, Madame Curie, Nobel laureates by the bundle, the list goes on and on of great men and women who have attributed their success directly to their intuition," writes Kehoe.

Shakti Gawain (author of *Creative Visualization*) says in her book *Living in the Light*,

> In this new world/new age, there is an understanding, a knowingness that there is a higher intelligence, a creative power or energy which is the source and substance of all existence. The words and concepts that have been used to describe this power are innumerable. Some names currently used in our culture are: God, Higher Power, Spirit, I Am, Source, Cosmic Intelligence, The Universe, The Light. The words we choose to describe it are merely the labels that suit us best. The word God has so many confusing connotations. Frequently, people associate it with early religious training which is no longer meaningful to them.

Once we acknowledge a higher power, the obvious question arises. How can we contact this power or gain access to it? This knowingness can be accessed through what we usually call our intuition. By learning to listen to and act on our intuition, we can directly connect to the higher power of the universe and allow it to become our guiding force. It is up to each of us to tune in and focus on the energy available to us. Gawain says that trusting your intuition is "a form of channeling," being in touch with and bringing through the wisdom and creativity of our own deepest source. When we are tuned in to the spirit within and allow ourselves to follow our intuition, things turn out right for us, and we experience joy, power, love, and peace. "Be conscious of the process. It is a wonderful way to live. We have a common power source and the same creative energy flows through each of us."

Françoise Tibika explains it well in her book *Molecular Consciousness: Why the Universe Is* Aware *of Our Presence*, which is filled with solid science as well as much novel philosophical thought, "Science deals only with phenomena that can be measured, and intuition is never part of an equation. Many scientists prefer to ignore what cannot be measured; many others even deny the existence of what cannot be measured."

We should bear in mind that as science progresses, phenomena that we cannot understand or quantify today may become measureable in the future, as discussed in chapter 14, "The New Science."

It is believed that Mozart, who wrote his music spontaneously and (seemingly) effortlessly, received it through intuition. He claimed that he received his inspiration from *within*.

A more recent example of someone who derived tremendous personal power through his strong connection to Spirit was Walter Russell (1871–1963).

Russell was born in the United States. He attended school until the fourth grade, and at the age of ten, he was put to work because of family problems. Despite his lack of education, he was able to master whatever he set his mind to. He became a master painter, sculptor, musician, architect, scientist, author, and philosopher. His works of art, the buildings he designed, and the outstanding monuments he sculptured are all still standing and admired. The real estate ideas he proposed are valued to this day. In science, he co-pioneered the prediction of the isotopes of hydrogen (deuterium and tritium), which lead to the discovery of heavy water. He also discovered two chemical elements, which he named uridium and urium (now called neptunium and plutonium). These elements were subsequently used by others to make the atomic bomb.

Russell believed that all knowledge comes from Source and is available to everyone. We simply have to plug into it. "Inspiration and intuition is the language of Light through which men and God intercommunicate."

Because of his extraordinary talents and achievements, Walter Russell has been called "the Modern Leonardo."

Russell demanded mastery of himself in all things—even in sports. He became a skilled horseman and a champion skater (winning three first-place prizes in figure-skating at the age of sixty-nine against competitors that were younger than thirty.) He moved from talent to talent without any preparation, explaining his genius as the result of being intimately connected to the universal intelligence (or God). He believed that the key to mastery is to be conscious of one's *desire* and focusing one's thought energy in the direction of that desire. He believed that man has unlimited power as long as he understands the principle of balance in natural law. "The underlying principle of Balance in Nature's One Law is equality of interchange between the pairs of opposites in any transaction in Nature." He extended this principle to the world of business, saying that equal interchange of goods and service between buyer and seller is key and must be written into the business code of ethics.

In 1921, Russell was divinely inspired to write the book *The Message of the Divine Iliad*. He received the information through *divine inspiration* and completed the book over a period of thirty-nine days. It was published without a single word needing to be changed in the original manuscript. "The language of that divine message was not mine. I could never have written such rhythmic essence of knowledge, not have created its exalted style," he said about his book.

A concise but excellent description of Russell's life and achievements can be found in the book *The Man who Tapped the Secrets of the Universe* by Glenn Clark.

***

The intuitive mind is a sacred gift and the
rational mind is a faithful servant.
We have created a society that honors the servant
and has forgotten the gift.

—Albert Einstein

Many scientists, medical professionals, and people from all walks of life find it impossible to believe that we are spiritual beings living in the physical world for short periods at a time. People like Eben Alexander, a neurosurgeon, had always wanted to believe in God and an afterlife, but his scientific mind strongly doubted that such things could exist. He knew that the brain is merely a machine that produces consciousness. His knowledge of the brain left little room for the continuing existence of a personality (or soul) after the brain stopped functioning. Then one day, he suddenly came down with an extreme illness that left him in a coma. He had contracted bacterial (E. coli) meningitis, a rare disease that attacks parts of the brain and causes unconsciousness. It is very rare in adults (less than one in ten million of the world's population contracts it annually), especially in the absence of any head trauma or other medical condition. He had a rare case of the disease that no one could explain the origins of. It did not respond to treatment.

Sometime during his seven-day period of unconsciousness, Alexander had a near-death experience (NDE) that he describes in detail in his book *Proof of Heaven*. "While I was in a coma my brain hadn't been working improperly. *It hadn't been working at all.* The part of my brain that years of medical school had taught me was responsible for creating the world I lived and moved in, was down, and out. And yet despite all of this, I had been alive, and aware, *truly aware.*"

Alexander had heard and read about near-death experiences but had never been open to the idea that something survives the death of the body. He wasn't even skeptical about the subject. He says, "Most skeptics aren't really skeptics at all. To be truly skeptical, one must actually examine something and take it seriously. And I, like many doctors, had never taken the time to explore NDEs. I had simply 'known' they were impossible. However, what I'd experienced was more real than the house I was in, more real than the logs burning in the fireplace. Yet there was no room for that reality in the medically trained scientific worldview that I'd spent years acquiring."

During his out-of-body experience, he found himself in a beautiful, incredible dream world—except it wasn't a dream. Alexander considered a number of neuroscientific hypotheses to explain what he had experienced. He concluded that even though he didn't know where he was or what he was, he *knew* that this place he suddenly found himself in was completely real.

In his book, Alexander describes his experiences while he was on the other side. He had many questions, and the answers came instantly but in a way that bypassed language. He saw that there are countless higher dimensions, but they cannot be known or understood from the earth plane. He was able to instantly and effortlessly understand concepts that would have taken years to fully grasp in a normal earthly life. The knowledge he acquired is stored, and it is with him still to this day. He learned and experienced many other things, and like others who have had NDEs, the unconditional love and acceptance that he experienced on his journey is the most important discovery he has ever made. "In the last analysis the only thing that truly matters is love. Love is, without a doubt, the basis of everything."

Usually, on returning to their physical body after an out-of-body experience, the person is able to describe what was happening around his bed in the hospital ward or what happened outside of the room where his body was lying or the panic of the doctors in the operating theater. On hearing these descriptions, doctors are always incredulous since they supposedly *know* that the patient was not alive at the time that they were desperately working to revive him. All the people who have near-death experiences report that they crossed over into another dimension or became aware of another realm of existence. Everyone who has had a NDE reports experiencing a divine presence, profound comfort, and unconditional love. Like Alexander, they report communicating with God during these journeys, not with words but rather through thought.

Dr. Alexander's truth is that *our spiritual self* is more real than anything we perceive in this physical realm and that it has a divine connection to the Creator.

Readers who are interested in delving more deeply into the subject of near-death and out-of-body experiences, evidence of the afterlife, and related topics are encouraged to consult the reading list at the back of Eben Alexander's book *Proof of Heaven*. It provides close to a hundred references to publications on the subject matter.

The term *near-death experience* was coined by psychiatrist Dr. Raymond Moody. He became interested in the subject of the afterlife after a psychiatrist friend told him he believed he had traveled into another plane of existence while being clinically dead for nine minutes. Moody began documenting similar reports by other people who had experienced clinical death.

After talking with more than a thousand people who had had these experiences, Moody became convinced that there is a life after death. "I must confess in all honesty, I have absolutely no doubt, on the basis of what my patients have told me, that they did get a glimpse of the beyond."

Moody's investigations into the afterlife were recorded in his book *Life after Life*, which sold more than thirteen million copies.

***

The remaining part of this chapter describes very briefly the experiences of people who have connected with friends and loved ones who have passed away. This is done with the aid of a *medium*. A medium is a person who brings through the essence of a departed person, allowing verbal communication between the latter and the living person who is seeking the connection. (More information about mediums is available in chapter 13, "Teachings from the Other Side.")

Throughout recorded history there have been people who had contact with worlds beyond the known universe. They have been called by various names—prophets, psychics, mediums, shamans, seers, oracles, channels, healers (Roman and Packer, 1987).

The first book I ever read on this subject was *The Life Beyond Death* by Arthur Ford, who researched reports about communication with the world of spirit and the subject of "life after life." He concluded that *our consciousness is indestructible and continues to live after physical death.*

The second book I read on the subject of communication with the world of spirit was called *The Other Side* by American attorney James Pike. Pike became a naval intelligence officer in World War II and then a bishop of the Episcopal church. After his son committed suicide, he began to notice strange phenomena in his apartment, specifically poltergeist phenomena (where physical objects move spontaneously, disappear and reappear, etc.). Pike believed that these were signs that his dead son was trying to contact him. He went to see a medium who was able to make a connection between Pike and his son, and they communicated many times. Pike usually took someone with him to these meetings as a witness, and he recorded everything that was said. He spent a great deal of time researching psychic phenomena and putting several mediums to the test, trying to confirm whether the contact was genuine. He was unable to prove unequivocally that there is indeed life after death, but he states at the end of his book the *he believes* there is.

A well-known medium who connects people with friends and family who have passed away is John Edward. The commnunication coming through from *the other side* may include information of a personal nature, the details of which are known only to the deceased and to the one seeking the connection (for example, a nickname or a special event that occurred). This serves as proof for the living person that the communication is authentic. Edward has a unique way of connecting people and transmitting information from the other side. His great skill as a medium has been witnessed by millions in the two television series *Crossing Over* and *Cross Country*. In these shows he works with an audience, bringing information from friends and loved ones to individuals in the group before him. The messages he presents are usually comforting for those who receive them.

Edward tells us that "when we lose a loved one, their physical body ceases to exist, but their soul and the essence of who they truly are lives on. We are still able to connect with that consciousness of love, and we don't need a medium's help to do it."

Edward is a Catholic who prays every day and before every public appearance as a psychic. He says, "Praying opens me spiritually, helps me connect with my spirit guides, and allows me to conduct my own dialogue with God whenever and wherever I want." Edward refers to his guides as a source of divine wisdom that assist him in creating and manifesting. But spirit guides are not there to do things for us. We still have to make our own choices.

More information about John Edward and his work can be found at www.johnedward.net and from his books, *Infinite Quest*, *Afterlife*, *Crossing Over*, and others. They are all informative works in which he describes his life as a psychic and teaches interesting aspects of this field. Edward also consults privately, working one-on-one with people who wish to connect with loved ones who have passed.

Another gifted medium who connects people with deceased loved ones is James Van Praagh. He describes mediums as "people who have a gift of being able to access the metaphysical plane effortlessly, and transmitting information from the other side, either verbally or in writing."

In his book *Heaven and Earth*, Van Praagh explains that "Spirit communication is like speaking a foreign language. It involves the interpretation of images communicated to us through telepathic thought. Images have unchanging meanings, for instance, a car or house has a meaning attached to it that is clear to anyone no matter what language he speaks. Words are merely letters combined to make a sound and may not have the same meaning for everyone."

The medium must interpret the images, and sometimes he may misunderstand them. Van Praagh gives the example of a spirit using an object to identify herself—a necklace with a locket. The medium sees her touching her throat but does not see the locket. He interprets the picture as "something is the matter with her throat" and may convey to the living person that the deceased suffered throat problems when she died or may warn him to watch out for a throat problem. Van Praagh explains that "we must bear in mind that misinterpretation or misidentification of the images does not mean that we are not communicating with the spirit world. It means that we are not understanding the message correctly." (A spirit entity may identify himself in other ways. Perhaps he may describe a personal detail or use a nickname known only to a few people.) It is necessary to remember that spirits communicate from a dimension that vibrates at a faster frequency than ours, and they tend to send their impressions more rapidly than we are used to on earth. It's as if we are communicating across a vast chasm without the help of a simultaneous translator. That is why mediums must stay as focused as possible on the information a spirit is conveying. Often mediums speak very quickly because they are trying to keep up with the information that comes through as rapid *downloads* of concepts.

Referring to the telepathic thoughts that he receives, Van Praagh tells us, "As a mental medium, I 'read' these thoughts as feelings, visions, and auditory impulses. I am able to interpret these messages through a common energy that permeates and transcends all levels of existence. I identify it as the God Force energy. For lack of better words, this energy is love. Love is the ingredient that makes the communication on both ends strong and successful."

According to Van Praagh, we all have the ability to tap into the support of our spirit guides, angels, and loved ones on the other side. We can use our psychic awareness on a regular basis to help solve everyday problems. He tells us that we can all connect with the world of spirit by using and trusting our intuition. "Developing your own innate psychic awareness comes only with practice and purpose. It is a process of attunement. In essence you are fine-tuning an instrument, the instrument being your own sixth sense."

***

Because we have free choice always, guides cannot make decisions for us. Guides can support and encourage, they can provide counsel, but we must make our own decisions.

—Veronica, channeled through April Crawford

The following true story, which occurred in South Africa, is told by Jasper Swain, an attorney by profession, who lost his son in a car accident. After the death of his son, Mike, the father was urged by a friend to visit a medium. He was reluctant at first, but he became curious and eventually felt compelled to see her. The medium connected father and son. Initially, Mr. Swain was incredulous. He found it hard to believe that such a thing could happen. During their first conversation, Mike told his father that when the violent accident occurred, he was lifted out of his body and felt no pain or shock. He described in minute detail how the accident had happened, the people who were present immediately after, and the state in which his body was found. After hearing Mike describing the accident exactly as it had happened, the father became convinced that the communication was indeed real. Mike talked about death as a natural, painless process for the soul, which is simply transported to another level of existence. The energetic state of the person at the time of death (i.e., his level of *evolution* in terms of personal development) determines the level to which the soul is transferred after death. The soul arrives in an energetic state that is similar to that of its physical life. Mike explained it as follows: "While you are still on earth, your thought, your intentions, everything you do gives your soul a certain rate of vibration. Let's suppose your soul is vibrating in a fifty-megacycle band. When you die and manifest here, you would go straight to that part of our world that vibrates at fifty mega cycles. It all depends on your rate of vibration." Therefore, the kind of life we live when in the physical determines what awaits us on the other side. Mike described other worlds above his that were "even richer in light and happiness, where the vibrations are so refined that I cannot respond to them." The planes below are denser and dimmer. Mike describes his sense of freedom as his greatest joy there.

All of this is described in detail in the book *Heaven's Gift*, which was written by Mike's father, Jasper Swain.

In the above story, the father learned something from Mike about the communication process itself (between a living person and a departed soul). Mike described it as a matching of the vibrations.

> Before you could raise yourself up to this plane, you would have to raise your vibrations to the speed of mine. Likewise, when I need to regress myself back to your world, I have to reduce my vibrations to their lowest rate. This isn't easy Dad: some of it is downright painful. It's like putting on a straightjacket. I have to constrict myself more and more, like the Rabbit in Alice in Wonderland, until my vibrations are moving as slowly as yours. But I am one of the few here who have been able to manage it. I can move from my world to yours by my own free will. But I would say that ninety-five percent of the souls at this level are completely unable to manifest at the earth level.

Mike's description of the change in frequency that occurs in our nonphysical part when we pass over matches the teachings of Roman and Packer. "When you die you increase your frequency in such a way as to be invisible to the earth plane, but visible to other realities. As you increase your vibration, things that were invisible to you before become visible, and obstructions, such as walls, become transparent to you."

In Mike's conversations with his father, he conveyed his concern about the suffering that people go through when their loved ones die. He said that it is unnecessary for people to suffer so much pain when someone dies. "Whenever you grieve for someone you love, your sorrow is immediately transmitted to him in his new world—a most beautiful world – but he cannot come back to the earth plane to comfort his mourners. He hasn't had time to master the art of slowing down his vibrations until you can see him or hear him." Mike says that instead of grieving, people should send their love and kind thoughts for a calm journey and a happy arrival, and remember that the friend they have lost is secure in that world of "warmth and happiness."

A similar message about our response to the death of a loved one is found in *The Reconnection* by Eric Pearl, whose mother went through a near-death experience and told him what she learned about the futility of mourning for those who have died. "If there is one regret experienced by the spirits who had passed, it was the pain suffered by those they left behind. They want us to rejoice in their passing, because to die is to go back home, to be where we want to be. The grieving is for *our* loss, the loss of the place in our lives once occupied by that person. Our time on earth is but a snap of the fingers in our eternal consciousness, and we will all be together momentarily. This is how it is meant to be." Pearl's mother returned from her experience, knowing with certainty that there is a Supreme Being and that we return home when we die. That is where we come from, where we belong. She also learned with unequivocal clarity that we are placed on earth to learn lessons that make us more complete souls. "We have to live this plan out on this level before we're ready to go on to another level."

***

The common thread running through the previously outlined instances of communication across the physical-spiritual divide can be summarized as follows:

- We are vibrational beings.
- Death is not the end of our existence. The soul crosses over into another dimension or realm of existence.
- An *acclimation* occurs when we pass to the other side—an adjustment to a different energy level, a higher frequency.
- We are welcomed and reunited with loved ones who crossed over before us.
- The frequency range at which we vibrate on earth is lower than that in the higher dimensions, making it difficult for us to access the higher dimensions.
- In order to align with the world of spirit, we need to raise our vibration and tune in to a higher frequency (like tuning in to a specific radio station).
- Communication occurs as thought images and not through the use of language.
- Our spiritual self has a divine connection to the Creator, and is eternal.
- Love is the basis of everything. It is the only thing that truly matters.

To those who believe, no explanation is necessary.
To those who don't believe, no explanation is possible.

—Raymon Grace

***

Here are a few words about the well-known psychiatrist Elizabeth Kubler-Ross (1926–2004), who worked for many years with the terminally ill and learned a lot about dying from her patients. She also researched the phenomenon of near-death experiences.

I have read three of Kubler-Ross's books, and I recommend them to anyone who wants to know more about the process of dying from a professional (medical) point of view and from the mind of an understanding and compassionate doctor. She was a pioneer in the study of the terminally ill and first discussed the five stages of grief in her book *On Death and Dying,* which has been described as the most humanitarian work on care of the dying in the Western world. She also wrote *The Wheel of Life: A Memoir of Living and Dying,* and *Life Lessons* which was coauthored with David Kessler.

I like the following passage, which appears in Kubler-Ross's book *The Wheel of Life*:

> When we have passed the lessons we were sent to earth to learn, we are allowed to graduate. We are allowed to shed our body, which imprisons our soul the way a cocoon encloses the future butterfly, and when the time is right we can let go of it. Then we will be free of pain, free of fears and free of worries … free as a beautiful butterfly returning home to God … which is a place where we are never alone, where we continue to grow and to sing and to dance, where we are with those we loved, and where we are surrounded with more love than we can ever imagine.

Reincarnation and Past-Life Regression Therapy

American psychiatrist Brian Weiss is one of many professionals who uses hypnosis as a tool to help his patients overcome trauma, fear, anxiety, and other problems that rob them of living a normal life. Under hypnosis, his patients are able to access memories from early childhood and even as far back as the womb. This helps them (as well as the therapist) to understand the origins of the psychological disturbances and to treat them appropriately. In his book *Many Lives, Many Masters*, Dr. Weiss describes how a patient began to access memories of a previous life during a routine regression.

Weiss had always believed that the present life is all there is, and he was skeptical about the information that this patient was recalling. However, her past-life traumas seemed to hold the key to her recurring nightmares and anxiety attacks. Other information that she recalled turned out to be so specific and accurate that Weiss became convinced that we do indeed undergo repeated rebirth. The validation of the information that his patients brought forth from previous lives during these regressions and the profound effect on their recovery transformed Weiss into an ardent believer in reincarnation.

After his first (accidental) experience with a past-life regression, Weiss embarked on a new phase of his career and now uses past-life therapy to treat people with emotional disturbances and physical ailments that have an emotional origin. He has written a number of books describing what he learned from his patients' regressions into past lives. His latest book, *Miracles Happen*, is a fascinating collection of past-life recollections by people who underwent regressions facilitated by Weiss. The information they accessed during these sessions helped them to release old emotional wounds. In some cases this resulted in the relief of physical ailments that had bothered them for many years and which medical professionals had been unable to cure. "Since the body and the mind are interconnected, what heals one often heals the other" (Weiss).

Knowledge of previous life experiences obtained through past-life therapy often reveals patterns that illuminate our present challenges and spiritual paths. The insights gained during a regression may help one to better understand a problematic present-day relationship.

For example, a person experiencing a specific difficulty (such as coping with an unkind relative) may discover through past-life therapy that he himself was cruel to others in a previous life. It doesn't mean that this person is destined to remain in an abusive relationship for the rest of this lifetime. The goal is to learn the lesson and apply the new understanding or to *let go* of an emotional burden. The knowledge gained from a past life may shine light on a current situation, and since the cause does not exist now, we can let go of the *symptoms*.

An example taken from the previously mentioned book involves a person who is now a social worker caring for underprivileged people. She discovered that she had previous lifetimes of being destitute and experiencing great loneliness. The suffering she experienced in the past led her to choose a vocation in her present life that enables her to exercise her empathy for people in need.

It is believed that we choose the kind of life we want to live in each lifetime in order to learn certain lessons, and that we reincarnate together with souls who were part of previous incarnations. In many instances a person who features in the past-life recall as a parent, grandparent, sibling or authority figure may be recognized as an existing member of the present family or some other current relationship. In short, the same soul is with us now, but in a different "capacity." In *Miracles Happen*, Weis writes, "Throughout time, we will meet with our loved ones again and again, either on the other side or back here in the physical state. We are all the same. We have been all races, all religions, all colors, both sexes, and many nationalities, because we have to learn from all sides. We are souls, and at the soul level we do not possess such outer transient characteristics. If everyone were to grasp this concept, racism would instantly disappear."

From his work Weiss concludes, "The ultimate lesson is that of unconditional love. We keep incarnating to learn this great truth in all its manifestations."

***

Sadly, love is a four-letter word that carries as
much interpretation baggage as "God."
—Source unknown

***

Edgar Cayce, considered by many to be the greatest clairvoyant of the twentieth century, didn't believe in reincarnation. When he heard a transcript of his own words uttered under trance, stating that people are reborn in different bodies, he was shocked and dismayed. (Cayce was a trance medium, a term described in chapter 13.) The concept of reincarnation was alien and repulsive to his conscious belief as a Christian (Presbyterian) who taught Sunday school and read the Bible daily. He became fearful that his subconscious faculties had been taken over by the devil, but with time he came to accept reincarnation, realizing that it did not call into question the teachings of Jesus Christ.

Cayce used his psychic powers mainly for *healing*, but over the next twenty-one years, he gave 2,500 *past-life readings*. He described personal histories spanning many incarnations in which the recurrent grouping of souls on earth occurred. Karmic patterns were revealed, often tracing present infirmity to deeds (or lack of deeds) in past lives. Cayce believed each person has subconscious access to skills accumulated in previous lives and is influenced by negative emotions such as hatred and fear from past lives.

***

My first encounter with the concept of reincarnation occurred relatively late in life, around my midtwenties. Most of us in the West belong to religions that do not teach about reincarnation, a belief that was part of the original Judeo-Christian doctrine.

Today most *Christians* are unaware that reincarnation was ever considered seriously by the church. But the fact remains that the early church fathers and the Christian Gnostics (an apostolic movement dedicated to preserving the esoteric teachings of Jesus Christ) accepted reincarnation as being consistent with Old and New Testament scripture.

In his book *The Case for Reincarnation*, Joe Fisher gives the history of the expulsion of reincarnation from Christian thought and theology.

In AD 312, the Roman emperor Constantine the Great converted to Christianity and established Christianity as the state religion. (Prior to this, it was considered an illegal cult whose members were hounded, abused, and exterminated.) "Eager to safeguard what he understood to be the authentic Christian message, Constantine called the Council of Nicaea in 325, to determine and define Christian orthodoxy. *It was decreed that we have two lives – one life in the natural body and one hereafter in the form of resurrection.* Bishops who disagreed with the Council's rulings were quickly deposed."

By 380, Christians whose beliefs differed from the orthodox view were chastised and accused of heresy, which became not merely sinful but a crime punishable by death. In 543, Emperor Justinian convened a synod in Constantinople, which condemned the teaching of reincarnation. Since then, the church has shunned the doctrine of rebirth.

Fisher speculates that the reason a belief in reincarnation angered the church authority may be that it caused offense since it encouraged its adherents to be self-reliant and thus minimized the sway of their totalitarian masters. "Believers in reincarnation were neither induced by promises of heavenly bliss nor intimidated by threats of hell fire. They didn't need priests to guide them along the straight and narrow path to God. This left the Church fiercely intolerant of professing Christians whose subservience could not be guaranteed."

"The church needed the whip of Judgement Day to keep the faithful in line. It was a matter of survival for the church not to allow belief in reincarnation to take hold among its followers" (Hans Holzer, quoted by Fisher). Departure from the official line was brutally punished, and a crusade of terror and slaughter continued throughout the following centuries as recorded in the annals of the Inquisition.

Reincarnation is an integral part of the *Jewish religion*, although many Jews are surprised to learn or may even wish to deny that reincarnation is an integral part of their belief system. Perhaps the reason for this is that the Torah's primary function is to teach us to live in harmony with God's will, and so the focus is on a *practical understanding* of mitzvoth and related Jewish values.

Although no direct reference to reincarnation is made in the scripture, the great *Kabbalists* explained its principles as follows: The soul is a spark of the divine. It is eternal, existing before it enters the body and continuing to live after the body is laid to rest. Although the soul's place of origin is the higher worlds, there is something that it can achieve in a body that it cannot achieve in the heavenly realms. In this world it acts as an abode for the divine. Usually a soul does not fulfill all the commandments in one descent, and so it must reincarnate repeatedly until it has fulfilled its mission of completing certain tasks, such as repaying a debt, or rectifying a sin.

Kabbalah teaches that souls reincarnate into specific sets of circumstances that are tailored to provide opportunities for rectifying previous sins. Sources: http://www.chabad.org/kabbalah/article_cdo/ aid/380599/jewish/Judaism-and-Reincarnation.htm and http://www. chabad.org/library/article_cdo/aid/361889/jewish/Reincarnation.htm.

In *Islam*, there are numerous references to reincarnation as given here:

"The person of man is only a mask that the soul puts on for a season. It wears its proper time, and then it is cast off and another is worn in its stead."

"God generates beings and sends them back over and over again till they return to Him."

"How can you make denial of Allah, who made you live again when you died, will make you dead again, and then alive again, until you finally return to him?"

The Quran alludes to the existence of soul groups, people who have emotional connections returning to life with those they have known before. "I tell you, of a truth, that the spirits which now have affinity shall be kindred together, although they all meet in new persons and names." Source: The Institute for the Integration of Science, Intuition and Spirit, accessible at www.iisis.net/index. php?page=semkiw-reincarnation-past-livesislam&hl=en US).

Past-life therapy confirms that mind and body share a close relationship and points to the idea that a psychological component exists for every physical disease. While it may take a lot of probing into successive lives to locate the source of a problem, once the relevant information is accessed from the subconscious, healing is usually rapid and dramatic. Nobody knows exactly how this remedial effect occurs, but it seems that the act of confronting and accepting long-trapped negativity in the psyche "provokes some alchemy of liberation." The ailment that is subsequently cured can be any form of phobia, addiction, allergy, and even cancer (Fisher).

Fisher relates case histories of young children, usually between the ages of two and four, who have memories of people and incidents of past lives. They recall names of people and places, details of the houses where they lived, and even the way they died. This may be shocking to uninformed parents, but when they investigate the history, most are relieved to find out that the stories are true and the child is not "possessed" by some evil force.

Verification of the details lends proof to the concept that reincarnation is a natural and worldwide occurrence. Investigators around the world report that individuals accurately describe race, class, clothing, and footwear worn across the centuries as well as the type of food and utensils used in their previous lives.

**

All of the information presented in this chapter supports the idea that we are more than purely physical beings and that there is no need to fear death. There is no death. There is a passing to another level of existence, a different dimension. It is a rebirth into the world of spirit.

> In a universe of quarks and black holes and eleven dimensions, "supernatural" doesn't mean what it used to. Then again, neither does "God."
>
> —Eric Pearl

Chapter 13

Teachings from the Other Side

We live in a three-dimensional world, meaning that we can move left and right, forward and backward, and up and down. Scientists have added another element, namely time as the fourth dimension. In Einstein's general theory of relativity, space and time are not separate entities but unified into a fourth dimension as space-time. Physicists tell us that in fact there are ten space-time dimensions as described in *string theory*. But it doesn't end there. *M-theory* proposes eleven space-time dimensions. Why can't we see or feel these extra dimensions? M-theory tells us that seven of the space dimensions are highly curved. They are curled up into a space of very small size, on a scale so small that we don't see them. This leaves us with the illusion that only the three large space dimensions that we are familiar with exist (Hawking and Mlodinow, 2011).

This chapter begins with the above brief and very superficial description of our physical reality (as the latest science understands it to be) made up of dimensions that are outside of our everyday experience. It is included here to draw comparison with the world of spirit, a dimension that is *hidden* from us just as the seven space dimensions mentioned above are hidden from us, yet they do exist, according to the experts.

People who have undergone near-death experiences relate spending time in dimensions beyond our earthly ones. It is as if a wall separates us from the spiritual realm. Some sources call it a *veil*. This summons the image of a thin barrier which could be almost transparent and may even be lifted. Indeed, Kryon tells us that in this new age of greater awareness and higher consciousness, the veil is being lifted and that we are getting glimpses of what exists on the other side of it.

Channeled Information

One way of connecting with the world of spirit is through a process called *channeling*, in which contact is made with other levels of reality.

In the previous chapter titled "Spiritual Connection," I describe a number of cases of people communicating with deceased loved ones through a *medium*—a person who is able to bring forth messages from the spiritual essence of people who have passed over. Here I describe cases of communication with *other* nonphysical entities or higher beings, such as spirit guides or angels (beings that may or may not have lived on earth). They raise the veil slightly to give us a glimpse of the world of spirit, which is our destination once we leave our familiar earthly plane.

Mediums have the gift of being able to access the metaphysical plane effortlessly. They transmit information from the other side, either verbally or in writing. There are basically two kinds of mediums, namely (1) those who bring forth the information while in a trance state and are unaware of the words/ideas that they are transmitting (and who often do not remember anything that was said during the channeling session and are thus called *trance mediums*) and (2) those who remain fully aware and remember the information that they receive and transmit (and who are called *conscious mediums*).

For some people, this may require a stretch of the imagination as this is a subject we are not normally exposed to. We often hear or read about negative reports involving charlatans who dabble in these activities for money and are not genuine seekers of truth or connection with the other side.

The person who channels is not controlled by anyone or anything. Rather he allows the information to flow through his physical faculties—voice and intellect. He receives the information as "packets" of concepts or images that he has to decipher and translate into verbal language. Some channels transfer the information in written form rather than the spoken language.

The following section describes information that has been received from high-level guides whose purpose in communicating with humans is to give guidance and teach us about the reality beyond our three-dimensional world. The spiritual guides/teachers whose messages are given here are the ones I am familiar with from the media, but there are many others sending information for the benefit of mankind.

The Teachings of Orin and DaBen

Orin and DaBen are spirit guides who describe themselves as "beings of light" that exist in the higher dimensions. Their goal is to assist us in opening to these dimensions so that we can more easily connect to our own guides and receive information that will enable us to develop and evolve. Their teachings are transmitted through Sanaya Roman and Duane Packer, who have written *Opening to Channel*. This book explains channeling and how to discriminate between high-level guides and less-evolved entities, and determine whether or not the advice we receive from a guide is trustworthy.

These authors pass on their knowledge of channeling from Orin and DaBen to anyone who is interested in becoming a channel (another word for medium). People who begin to *connect* to the world of spirit in this way report undergoing positive changes in their lives as a result of their newfound connection. They acquire clear vision of their life purpose, a higher trust in their inner wisdom, and new attitudes that are beneficial in their day-to-day living.

Orin and DaBen define channeling as "building a bridge to the higher realms—a loving, caring, purposeful collective higher consciousness that has been called God, the All-That-Is, or the Universal Mind. It helps you to connect to a constant, steady source of inspiration and information." They tell us that we are living in a very important time for the earth and that many high-level guides are present and want to assist us in order to serve mankind. In every case, the messages transmitted during channeling are messages of hope and empowerment for humans, with information to be used for the good of the person receiving them or for the common good of mankind. "As high-level guides we are here to make a difference, to serve mankind."

Information about these spirit guides and the books and courses provided by the above-mentioned authors can be found at www. orindaben.com.

The Teachings of Kryon

Kryon is the name given to a group of spiritual entities, a "soul group" that is part of and represents the Whole (God). The messages come through as though from one *being*, meaning that the language used is in the first person.

Kryon tells us that he comes to be of service to humanity in our quest to create peace on earth and that we are ready to receive the teachings that Spirit wants to give us. We should open ourselves to things we don't know as we tend to believe only what we have been taught. This is "our" truth—but the universal truth is outside of our shield of tradition.

The teachings of Kryon come to us through Lee Carroll, an American engineer who has been transmitting messages from Kryon since 1989. All the teachings remain relevant to us today, even the earliest ones. (Kryon speaks through other people besides Lee Carroll, but only Carroll's channelings are discussed in this book.)

Carroll receives the communications in a form that is independent of language. The messages come as ideas and *thought packages* that Carroll translates into words. It is difficult to explain, much like trying to explain color to a sightless person.

At first, Lee Carroll did not believe in any of this "esoteric stuff." His wife would drag him "kicking and shouting" to her spiritual meetings in the hope that he would become interested. He would sit at the back of the audience, pouting and sulking, until one day he was *chosen* by an angelic energy called Kryon to engage in channeling. He refused. As he did not believe in such things, he remained aloof until he finally agreed to give it a try. Once he began to accept the possibility that this may be a genuine connection with Spirit, he allowed the communication to come through and began to channel Kryon's messages. He was profoundly touched by the experience. He accepted the gift, and with time he developed expertise in how to interpret and translate the messages. Today Lee Carroll and Kryon are known worldwide, and their messages are translated into many languages. They were invited six times (from 1995 to 2007) to channel at the UN headquarters in New York by the UN Staff Recreation Council. These events were attended by UN staff, delegates, members of the Society of Enlightenment and Transformation (SEAT), and invited guests.

Kryon defines channeling as *the divine, inspired words (or energy) of God as imparted to Humans through Humans. Channelling provides a portal for connection with the Creative Source.*

"The above definition is what channelling actually IS. That means that not only were most of the sacred scriptures of the planet (all religions) channelled originally, but also much artwork and music too. It is absolutely commonplace, but like so many other re-emerging processes in the New Age, it has a stigma about being strange. God did not write the Bible … humans did, while divinely inspired" (Carroll).

Carroll claims that God did not stop speaking to humans two thousand years ago. To think that God stopped communicating is to deny our own divinity or to assign some special sacredness to the past. He explains that channeling is often misunderstood as something spooky and weird. Some people even think it is evil and don't want anything to do with it. They would rather stick with information that isn't channeled (they think).

> We have been used to having authorized men and women of God passing information to us—not the common folk. Anyone can channel, and Spirit is not proprietary in this regard. It's for all Humans, and not just a few.

> Many men and women are sprouting verbiage these days, calling it inspired. How can you tell if it's real or not, since there is no organization telling you who is "OK" and who is not? Not all channeling is given with *pure intent*. Therefore some is real, and some is not, and you should be able to tell the difference when you hear or read it. Is it really from spirit? (Carroll).

Carroll teaches how to discern whether a channeled message is genuine or not, how you can tell the difference between a *real* channel and egocentric information given by someone who is not truly connecting with Spirit.

Here are some guidelines for discerning the authenticity of channeled messages.

1. There will always be useful information for everyone. Beware of the channel that gives information for only a few or for a special group. It must be useful for *all* of humanity. This is an area of discernment allowing us to know we are hearing the truth.

2. The message should be uplifting and empowering, not one of fear, not one that drags us down. This is a staple of God energy. Every recorded appearance of an angel before a human being has begun with "Fear not!"

3. Spirit (God) will never channel a message that asks us to give up our free will. Free choice is what our experience on earth is all about. It drives our future.

4. Spirit will never give us a message that violates our integrity. We must feel comfortable with it. It must ring true.

5. Spirit will never represent a particular channeler as being the only source. There are many channels of Spirit, and their information is coordinated to create a bigger picture. They will never represent themselves as the only source of information.

6. The information is normally new. Beware of the channel that simply rehashes the old. New information is necessary. It is the entire reason for the channel.

7. Channeled information should present spiritual solutions. Solutions to life challenges on earth (via new information) is the purpose of channeling.

***

The teachings of Kryon cover topics such as

- human biology;
- our place in the universe;
- historical events relating to mankind, the earth, and the universe;
- science and the physics of the universe;
- belief in God;
- reincarnation;
- the need for compassion in our world;
- the current struggle between the forces of darkness and light;
- various problems facing humanity; and
- our free choice to accept the teachings or not.

Kryon explains that Spirit does not foretell the future for the world. Man decides the future according to the choices he makes in the present. Kryon sees potentials based on the present state of affairs, but the future depends on man's intent and actions. Furthermore, he explains that spiritual entities and guides never interfere in people's lives. They may give guidance but may not tell us what to do. They honor our free choice.

Kryon describes the changes taking place on the planet and in human consciousness. Despite the present sorry state of society, Kryon's vision for the future is one filled with hope. The potential for change is high, and most of it is moving in the right direction. Changes that have taken place on the planet, such as a shift in the magnetic grid, affect our biology and the consciousness of humanity. We are told to watch out for the new children—they are born different. They are more self-aware. They remember where they came from and may even remember lessons from previous lives. They have a wisdom that we adults took a very long time to develop.

The teachings of Kryon are always brought to us in a warm and loving way with a great understanding of the human condition. He tells us repeatedly that we are never alone.

Kryon's main message is that we are here to grow/mature into balanced, compassionate human beings connected to Spirit. The ultimate goal is to evolve a higher consciousness and achieve peace on earth. He says that the potential to achieve peace is high. Yes, there will be disagreements between nations, but we will not kill one another because of them. War will no longer be an option, and the few countries who want to choose war will not be supported by the rest of the world.

All the information about the Kryon teachings can be found at www. kryon.com. The section titled "Channelling" contains information for newcomers to the site.

The Teachings of Seth

Seth is a nonphysical entity internationally known as a spiritual teacher who spoke through the American author Jane Roberts (1929–84). Roberts received almost two thousand messages dictated by Seth while she was in a trance. She produced thousands of pages containing information on creative living, answers to life's questions, and the grandeur of our human potential. The manuscripts are kept at the Yale University Library of Manuscripts and Archives, and many books containing the channeled information have been published. The Seth books have sold more than seven million copies and have been translated into eleven languages. These books were published from 1966 to 2003.

Jane Roberts describes how channeling started for her suddenly one day when she was at home, "A fantastic avalanche of radical, new ideas burst into my head with tremendous force. It was as if the physical world were really tissue-paper thin, hiding infinite dimensions of reality, and I was flung through the tissue paper with a huge ripping sound." When she "came to," Roberts found she had written a batch of notes that was subsequently published in her first book, *The Physical Universe as Idea Construction*. More than thirty Seth books were authored by Jane Roberts. They discuss a wide range of metaphysical concepts including the nature of God, the nature of the "Higher Self", the evolution of the soul, death and reincarnation, past lives, multidimensional reality, and the origens of the universe. These books are probably the most widely read channeled material of the past thirty years.

Roberts tells us that "a trance is a natural state, merely a matter of focusing one's consciousness, not unlike hypnosis." Her ability to reach such a state allowed a *bridge* between herself and Seth. Before this, Roberts had never had any interest in psychic phenomena. Nor did she believe in extrasensory abilities. One of Seth's messages to us is as follows: "I speak to you because yours is the opportunity to better world conditions and yours is the time. Do not fall into the old ways that will lead you precisely into the world that you fear. You are in essence, creative spiritual beings having an earthly experience." Seth's messages support the belief that communication with the world of spirit is benevolent to humans. The teachings of Seth are considered by some to be as important as the original teachings of Jesus.

Information about Seth's teachings can be found at www.sethlearningcenter.org and www.sethcenter.com.

The Teachings of Abraham

Abraham is the name a group of spiritual teachers from the nonphysical dimension. Their teachings are brought to us through the medium Esther Hicks.

The teachings of Abraham are about experiencing joy and well-being, and creating the life you want. They provide the original source material for the concept of the *Law of Attraction*, a concept that is sweeping the world.

The Law of Attraction can be briefly explained as follows: We are vibrational beings. Our vibration varies according to our thoughts, moods, and emotions. By paying attention to the way we feel, we get an indication of the frequencies we emanate. We attract to ourselves that which is in vibrational alignment with the frequency we emit. We attract whatever it is we give our attention to, and if we are in vibrational range, it will be drawn to us. If our thoughts and emotions are defeatist or gloomy, we will attract similar vibrations. The same occurs with positive thoughts and emotions. Set yourself into vibrational harmony with that which feels good. Once you realize what the receiving mode feels like, you can hold yourself in the frequency that is in harmony with the well-being you desire.

Focus your thoughts on what you desire and *delete* all negative thoughts, including doubts about achieving what you desire. The only reason that something that you want is not coming to you is that you are holding yourself in vibrational harmony with something other than what you want. This is the science of deliberate creation.

Esther Hicks holds workshops where people ask Abraham questions and receive the answers directly through her. Everything is documented and available as CDs, DVDs, and books. The book I have read and recommend is called *Ask and It Is Given*.

Some of the Abraham teachings may be summarized as follows: We are physical extensions of that which is nonphysical. The purpose of life is joy. We create everything in our lives with our thoughts. Anything that we can imagine is ours to be or do or have. We cannot die. We are everlasting life.

All the teachings can be accessed at http://www.abraham-hicks.com.

Other Teachings

Edgar Cayce is a famous American medium who lived in the period 1877–1945. People would consult him for help with personal and medical problems. Cayce always gave accurate information on holistic health and the treatment of illness, and because he did this while in a deep trance, he became known as the "sleeping prophet." His responses came to be called "readings," and they were all recorded by his secretary. Hundreds of books have been written about him and his medical advice, which was sound and effective. Even today individuals from all walks of life receive relief from illnesses thanks to the information given in the readings, despite the fact that some readings were given as far back as a hundred years ago. Apparently, Cayce was quite religious. In fact, he is reported to have read the entire Bible every year!

Information about Cayce and his readings is available at www. edgarcayce.org, which includes details of the Cayce Association for Research and Enlightenment (ARE).

April Crawford, who has been receiving messages from an angelic entity called *Veronica* for many years, is a deep-trance medium. April describes what happens when she channels, "Over the years I have become adept at removing myself from the process (of channeling). At first I was totally not aware and it bothered me. After being given access to the conversations, I see clearly how much I am not needed. Knowing that the work is clear and helpful allowed me to consciously let go. I am just the vessel, not necessary to the information." It has been explained that it is never April that is speaking during deep-trance sessions. It is always 100 percent whoever is coming through. Usually, it is Veronica who comes through, but it could also be one of many others. Typically, these channelings are warm and comforting. In one of the messages, Veronica tell us, "Be aware everyday of your connection with Spirit. Make time for the relationship in your busy day. Stay connected even in the most dire moments. Stay focused in the strength of your soul. It will provide the necessary means to be strong on every level." Veronica acknowledges that living in a physical reality often causes us to disconnect from the soul. "If you find yourself detached for whatever reason, it is important to take steps to reconnect internally. If you are off-course, use your truth as a compass to guide you back to your true North."

I particularly like the following advice given by Veronica via April Crawford: "If you are currently dissatisfied with your life for any reason take the time to examine your thoughts. If you are truthful with yourself you will be able to see the process that has brought you to where you are now. How do you change it? Examine how you think. Your thought creates your reality. Thoughts are the most powerful tool in the universe and they are right there in your head. It is within your power."

Veronica's messages can be accessed at www.aprilcrawford.com and in the book *Heavenly Match* by April Crawford and Veronica.

A Course in Miracles

There is a publication called *A Course in Miracles* (often referred to by its acronym ACIM), which has become a treasured work of inspiration and guidance to the many people who have studied it. Many readers claim that it changed their lives. ACIM provides daily lessons and a system for self-study that shows us how to retain our wholeness and our power, and identify ourselves as divine beings. It teaches that relationships are the key to healing.

ACIM has sold more than two million copies worldwide. It was written from 1965 to 1977 via channeled, automated writing by psychology professor Helen Schucman (1909–1981), who believed that she received the teachings directly from Jesus.

I personally have not been drawn to ACIM. It is written in the style of a religious book and does not resonate with me. I include it here because so many people report that it has transformed their lives for the better, so it may be useful for some readers. However, I do identify with the writings of Marianne Williamson, whose life was changed by ACIM. She has written a book titled *A Return to Love*, which I have read, and through it I understood what ACIM is about. There is another author named Alan Cohen, who also transmits the teachings of ACIM through his publication *A Course in Miracles Made Easy*, which I have not read.

***

I expect that much of what is written in this chapter is not accepted by some readers as it is foreign to everyday experience and may seem to have no basis in reality. I compare the reluctance to accept paranormal phenomena with the reluctance that some scientists have to accept quantum theory (described in chapter 14). The latter too requires a stretch of the imagination.

The history of science contains many changes of ideas and theories, and the following two examples show how biased our modern science can be against anything that does not have a proven mechanism:

1. Our present understanding of the nature of light illustrates the changing nature of scientific dogma as new knowledge emerges. Early experiments led Newton to believe that light consists of particles (called photons). Later, however, it was found that under certain circumstances light behaves as a

wave. In the twentieth century, Einstein showed that light behaves as both particle and wave, a duality that is foreign to everyday experience but is now accepted as fact.

2. In the early twentieth century, a lively debate was raging between geologists over a proposed theory concerning the movement of the continents. From the mapping of the oceans and the land on the earth, some geologists concluded that all the continents were once part of a single land mass. Somehow the big mass had broken up and "drifted" apart. They said that the outlines of the continents fit into one another just like a puzzle. The proponents of this theory were ridiculed by some of the scientists because everyone *knew* that continents could not move. How could continental rock plow through the much denser rock that makes up oceanic crust? It was nonsense. Yet around the mid-twentieth century, with the development of new instruments and ocean-going research vessels, geophysical evidence indicated that the ocean floor does indeed move. This new evidence made it clear that continental drift was feasible, and the mechanics of plate tectonics unfolded (1965–67). This revolutionized the earth sciences as it explained a diverse range of geological phenomena as well as the fossil records found in various locations. The Continental Drift theory became scientific fact almost overnight.

***

I relate the above historical facts to illustrate how scientific thinking changes as new facts are revealed. Theories that had proven successful were later replaced by other equally successful theories based on wholly new concepts of reality. The same evolution of ideas exists in matters relating to the connection between mind and matter, intuition, metaphysics, and the world of spirit.

For centuries we have followed the teachings in our scriptures. When they were given, they were appropriate for the *audience* of the time. Mankind was (and is) an unruly species as illustrated by our history. The old teachings served us for millennia; however, man has progressed, and today many people regard the scriptures as quaint mythology. The information being transmitted to us from the world of spirit in this new age may serve as an *upgrade* to the ancient scriptures. God has not changed, but the world has.

The information that is currently coming to us through channeling does not contradict or replace the old teachings. Neither do the channelings encourage us to reject any of the scriptures we hold sacred. Rather, they are timely and suited to the world we live in now. We can regard these channeled teachings as the new inspired "messages from the angels" transmitted to us through human channels just as the scriptures are the inspired words of God that were recorded by humans long ago. Today, however, we are getting these messages without the external phenomena that accompanied some of the ancient ones (such as burning bushes or chariots in the sky). Perhaps we do not need such displays in order to be convinced of the authenticity of the messages.

Kryon tells us that mankind is graduating from the age of "schoolyard bullying" and maturing into a more evolved level that exhibits greater *wisdom*. The new energy in this new age facilitates this process, which has already started but will take a long time to complete.

Kryon foresees the evolved human to be _more_ *balanced, understanding, aware, slow to anger, peaceful, wise, compassionate, and generous of spirit*. Compassion is the key, and peace is the goal.

Would anyone argue against this as a good destination for mankind?

The new science tells us that everything is interconnected or entangled, and that includes us. More and more people are opening up to this idea of communion between people, between us and nature, between us and our planet. For some, this includes our connection to a higher power that exists beyond the physical. Our search for meaning leads us to this place.

Despite the information overload and our virtual, online connection to one another, the need for *real human contact* remains, as it was before the Information Age. Our inner lives have not evolved at the same speed as our technology. Similarly, the need to connect with our spiritual source exists today as it has throughout our human history.

Kryon says the Creative Source is within us, whether we accept this as a fact or not, and we have free choice regarding the acceptance or rejection of connecting with the divine.

***

A common thread that runs through all of the teachings from the other side can be summarized as follows:

- The angelic entities that channel messages to us love humanity.
- They come in service to mankind. Their goal is to teach and enlighten us.
- Humanity is ready to receive these teachings.
- Different spirit entities have different styles of communication, and some may specialize in specific "subjects".
- Communication is achieved via *concept packages* as thought energy, which has to be interpreted and translated by the person receiving it.

- The world of spirit is accessible to us, especially in moments of tranquility.
- We can commune with our spiritual guides for help and guidance, but it may take time and practice to achieve this.
- Spirit guides help us to understand the issues that trouble us, but they do not solve our problems for us.
- Spirit guides respect our free choice and never interfere in our lives.
- We are vibratory beings, and we broadcast signals that match our emotional states.
- The frequencies we broadcast align with and attract similar or matching frequencies.
- We create our reality with our minds and thoughts.
- We are spiritual beings, extensions of the Creative Source.
- The Creative Source is within us. We are never alone.

***

We are not Human Beings having a spiritual experience,
we are spiritual beings having a human experience.

—Pierre Teilhard de Chardin, scientist and Jesuit priest

***

For many people, the concepts described in this chapter represent a mythology that belongs with fairy tales. However, just as there are theories in science that seem absurd at first but eventually gain credence, similarly, the subject of spirituality is gaining acceptance as more evidence of personal experiences comes to light.

In science, theories are proposed about things we cannot see or experience. Good examples are *string theory* and *M-theory*, which were mentioned at the beginning of this chapter. These are based on space-time having ten (or eleven) dimensions instead of the usual four, with seven of the dimensions being curled up into such a small space that we cannot see them.

I find these ideas highly speculative and difficult to accept. Many concepts in science have not been proven and remain as theories—many of them being about things that are totally foreign to our everyday experience. Are they ridiculed to the extent that ideas regarding spirituality are ridiculed? No, perhaps because they are attached to the word *science*, which in many circles gives them more legitimacy than the word *spirit*.

> It is hard to go beyond what you know.
> You do not know what (it is that) you don't know.

—Kryon. (words in backets added to enhance clarity, HB)

Part 4

The Bigger Picture

Chapter 14

The New Science

Until the advent of modern physics, it was thought that all knowledge of the world could be obtained through direct observation as perceived by our senses—that things are as they seem. But the success of modern physics and quantum mechanics has shown that this is not the case (Hawkins and Mlodinow, 2010).

Our understanding of nature and of the universe is based on the work of the great seventeenth-century physicist Isaac Newton. Newton's laws accurately describe the motion of all bodies in the universe from a grain of dust to galaxies. These laws reflect everyday experience in which material objects have an individual existence, can be located precisely, and follow definite paths. Newton's laws were the only laws known until Albert Einstein conceived his general theory of relativity.

By the beginning of the twentieth century, Newton's laws were found to be inadequate for describing nature at the atomic and subatomic level. Atoms and molecules behave in a manner that is different from our everyday experience. The new laws of quantum mechanics were developed and superseded Newton's laws in less than two decades.

Around the same time, Max Planck discovered that the energy of heat radiation is not emitted continuously but appears in the form of *energy packets*. Einstein called these packets *quanta* and recognized them as a fundamental aspect of nature. He postulated that light is made up of these quanta (or photons, which are particles that lack mass and travel at the speed of light). But … light was known to behave as waves too, which led to the hypothesis that light has a double nature, sometimes behaving like a wave and sometimes like small particles. This introduced a new concept in science—that of the *dual nature* of light.

This idea arose in 1909 thanks to an experiment carried out by G. I. Taylor. It is called the *double-slit experiment*, and it has become a classic. It expresses the central puzzle of quantum mechanics. The Nobel laureate in physics Richard Feynman pointed out that the entire mystery of quantum mechanics is in the double-slit experiment.

This experiment demonstrates that when a stream of photons passes through a thin wall with a slit in it, they hit the barrier behind the wall at specific points like tiny particles. When there are two slits in the wall and the photons pass through, an interference pattern is observed behind the thin wall. The stream of photons behaves as a wave.

Shortly after this discovery, another scientist named Louis de Broglie proposed that *matter* also has a double nature. Scientists responded with disbelief to this radical idea (that matter, like light, can be both wave and solid). A few years later, George Thomson showed that *electrons* also have a double nature!

It has been confirmed that this phenomenon occurs with photons, electrons, atoms, and even some molecules, including buckyballs (large spherical molecules consisting of carbon atoms). Thus, *wave-particle duality* became part of our understanding of nature.

This property of matter and of light is very strange. It seems impossible to accept that something can be at the same time a particle (i.e., an entity confined to a very small volume) and a wave (which is spread out over a large region of space). The above-mentioned experiment shows that *we* are the ones who determine how to see a photon or electron by deciding whether or not to open a slit.

The observer plays a crucial role in the world of quantum physics, where the physical world is divided into an *observed* system (e.g., atom, subatomic particle, an atomic process, etc.) and an *observing* system (the experimental apparatus and one or more human observers). "We cannot just observe without interfering. Quantum physics recognizes that to make an observation, you must interact with the object you are observing (for example, shining even a dim light on a tiny quantum particle in order to see it has an appreciable effect on it and changes the results of an experiment" (Hawkins and Mlodinow). Further, it was shown that the more the particles are observed, the greater the effect of the observer.

Einstein found this hard to believe and called it "spooky science," preferring to think that matter has an independent existence unrelated to human influence.

The amazing hypothesis of the dual nature of matter soon became an indisputable fact, but it required a mathematical juggling act. The equations from the classical physics of solids had to be combined with equations from the physics of waves. This was achieved thanks to the major contribution of physicist Erwin Schrodinger (Tibika).

In quantum theory, the observed systems are described in terms of *probabilities*. For example, we cannot say with certainty where an electron will be in an atom at a certain time. Its position depends on the attractive force binding it to the nucleus and the influence of the other electrons in the atom. These conditions determine a probability pattern that represents the electron's tendencies to be in various regions of the atom. In quantum theory these tendencies are expressed as probabilities. All the laws of atomic physics are expressed in terms of these probabilities.

> At the subatomic level, the solid objects of classical physics dissolve into wave-like patterns of probabilities, and these patterns, ultimately, do not represent probabilities of things, but rather *probabilities of interconnections.* As we penetrate into matter, nature does not show us any isolated "building blocks," but rather appears as a complicated web of relations between the various parts of the whole. These relations always include the observer in an essential way. In atomic physics, we can never speak about nature without at the same time, speaking about ourselves. *Quantum theory thus reveals a basic oneness of the universe.* (Capra).

Eben Alexander, a brain scientist whose understanding of the world changed after he had a near-death experience, observes that we see the universe as being full of separate objects (tables, chairs, people, and planets) that occasionally interact with one another but that nonetheless remain essentially separate. On the subatomic level, however, this universe of separate objects turns out to be a complete illusion. In the realm of the super small, every object in the physical universe is intimately connected with every other object. In fact, there are really no "objects" in the world at all, only vibrations of energy and relationships.

Fritjof Capra says the same thing, but being a theoretical physicist, he uses scientific jargon. "The recognition that mass is a form of energy eliminated the concept of a material substance from science and with it also that of a fundamental structure. Subatomic particles are not made of any material stuff; they are patterns of energy. When we observe them, we never see any substance, nor any fundamental structure. What we observe are dynamic patterns continually changing into one another—a continuous dance of energy."

***

Other more sophisticated experiments reveal even odder behavior of particles, such as quantum *entanglement*. Two particles that are generated from a single one will always remain *connected* even when they are separated by great distances. Anything that happens to one of the particles will also happen to the other simultaneously irrespective of space and time. This view of modern science was expressed by a leading physicist named David Bohm (1917–1992), who developed his *theory of the implicate order* to explain the bizarre behavior of subatomic particles. "Two subatomic particles that have once interacted can instantaneously respond to each other's motions thousands of years later when they are light-years apart." (Einstein called this "spooky action at a distance.")

This was illustrated relatively recently (in 1997) in an experiment conducted at the University of Geneva. Two particles were generated from a single particle and were separated by a vast distance within a specially designed instrument. It was found that when one of the particles was subjected to a change, the other particle responded as if it was still connected to the first.

Erwin Schrodinger, who won the Nobel Prize in physics in 1933, stated that entanglement is *the* characteristic trait of quantum mechanics. The significance of this phenomenon is extrapolated to the situation at the time of the birth of the universe. Before the Big Bang, all matter was tightly concentrated, occupying a very, very small space. After the Big Bang, the universe expanded and continues to expand, *but all the particles remain connected energetically.* By virtue of our common origin, the Earth and all life on it are made up of the same atoms that make up the cosmos. Since modern science has shown that *all is energy* (chapter 5) and that particles remain connected at the energy level, it follows that we (humans) are connected to one another, to the earth, and to everything else.

> When we look at any one thing in the world,
> we find it is hitched to everything else.

—John Muir, environmentalist, philosopher, and author

Summary of the Findings that Led to Quantum Theory

- There's a wave/particle duality of matter.
- Physical events are influenced by the observer.
- All matter is connected, entangled.
- The laws of physics are not universal. (Subatomic particles of high velocities behave differently from large, slow-moving objects.)

The quantum model of nature encompasses principles that contradict not only our everyday experience but our intuitive concept of reality too. In fact, great physicists such as Einstein and Feynman, had difficulty in completely accepting it. Feynman once wrote, "I think I can safely say that nobody understands quantum mechanics."

The *absurdity* of quantum theory is well described by Hans Christian von Baeyer in his article "Quantum Weirdness? It's All in Your Mind" (*Scientific American*, November 2015). "Unlike evolution and cosmology, whose truths have been incorporated into the general intellectual landscape, quantum theory is still considered (even by many physicists) to be a bizarre anomaly, a powerful recipe book for building gadgets but good for little else. The deep confusion about the meaning of quantum theory will continue to add fuel to the perception that the profound things it is so urgently trying to tell us about our world are irrelevant to everyday life and too weird to matter."

Quantum phenomena and their obscure mechanisms continue to arouse much debate in the scientific community, although some scientists accept quantum theory as fact. Hawkins and Mlodinow argue that quantum theory agrees with observations and state that "It has never failed a test, and it has been tested more than any other theory in science." This new theory opened new areas of research, one of which gave rise to the computer.

The scientists who do accept quantum physics' description of matter and the universe muse on what it all means regarding ourselves as part of the physical world. Tibika points out that as incredible as it might seem and in spite of all the knowledge that has accumulated, "the intrinsic nature of matter—which surrounds us and from which we are made—became, at the dawn of the twentieth century, one of the biggest enigmas of science. Made of a countless number of these enigmatic bits of matter, what are we? A cluster of particles? A bundle of Waves? Both?"

"Quantum theory was born only a few decades ago. It has hardly travelled beyond the doors of research institutions and hardly started to infiltrate in the public mind. This theory could launch the next big scientific revolution" (Tibika).

Undoubtedly, there are undiscovered laws of physics that will surprise scientists in the future and will help us to better understand the universe, our planet, and ourselves.

Our knowledge enables us to evaluate the extent of our ignorance.

—David Gross, Nobel laureate in physics (2004)

***

I believe that understanding the concept of *entanglement* is important as it affects us directly. Physicist and author Vlatko Vedral explains it well, "One strange consequence of entanglement is that entangled particles behave as a single entity, even when they are far apart. Entanglement binds together individual particles into an indivisible whole." It is independent of space and time.

This tells us that we are all connected.

***

Toward the end of the twentieth century, three important experiments involving *human DNA* were conducted. These have changed the way we view our role in the world.

Experiment 1: At the Russian Academy of Sciences, Vladimir Poponin carried out a series of experiments which were reported in a scientific paper in the United States in 1995. Poponin created a vacuum in a specially designed tube in which photons were distributed randomly. When he inserted human DNA into the tube, the photons became aligned with the DNA molecule. When the DNA was removed, the arrangement of the photons remained as if the DNA was still in the tube. This is called the *DNA phantom effect* and demonstrates that human DNA exerts an effect on its physical surroundings.

Poponin believed that "this discovery has tremendous significance for the explanation and deeper understanding of the mechanisms underlying subtle energy phenomena including many of the observed alternative healing phenomena."

Experiment 2: This experiment was carried out in the 1990s by scientists cooperating with the US military. DNA was isolated from human donor cells and placed in a separate room in the same building, a hundred feet away from the donor. The donor was subjected to various emotional stimuli in the form of video clips. As the donor experienced emotional peaks and valleys, the responses of the DNA were monitored (as electrical impulses). The DNA exhibited responses at exactly the same time as the donor experienced different emotional states. There was no time lag. When the donor and his DNA were separated by a distance of fifty miles, the results remained the same, indicating a previously unrecognized field or form of energy that is independent of time and space.

This experiment provides evidence that the human donor and his DNA remained connected on the quantum level over vast distances and that the energy from the donor's emotional state didn't travel anywhere because it was already everywhere.

Experiment 3: An American organization named the Institute of HeartMath, which focuses its research on the heart, examined the effect of human emotions on isolated DNA. Twenty-eight vials of DNA were given to twenty-eight researchers who had been trained to generate emotions by applying a powerful form of feeling known as coherent emotion (shifting one's awareness to the heart area and focusing on the emotions). When the researchers projected positive emotions such as gratitude, appreciation, and love, the DNA helix unwound slightly, becoming longer. Negative emotions such as fear, anger, jealously, and hatred caused the helix to tighten, becoming shorter. It was concluded that our emotions affect our DNA directly.

The conclusions derived from these three experiments include the following:

a. Human DNA exerts an effect on photons and thus on the stuff our world is made of.
b. Our thoughts and emotions directly affect our DNA (which affects the stuff our world is made of).
c. Thoughts and emotions influence matter directly and independently of time and space.
d. We remain connected to our DNA across small and large distances.
e. A type of energy exists that has not been previously recognized.

Gregg Braden believes these observed effects are transmitted through a *field of energy* that connects everything in the universe. This field is made up of an energy form that appears to be different from a conventional electrical field and has been referred to as "subtle energy."

The energy discovered in these experiments is so new that scientists have yet to agree on a name for it. In his book *The Divine Matrix*, Braden mentions names that have been used to describe this *energy field* and by whom, including

- *Intelligent Mind* (Max Planck, Nobel Prize for his work on quantum theory, 1918);
- *Nature's Mind* (Edgar Mitchell, former Apollo astronaut);
- *Quantum Hologram* (Michio Kaku, physicist and coauthor of superstring theory); and
- *Divine Matrix* (Gregg Braden, scientist and author).

This energy field is everywhere all the time. It does not have to be produced in one place and sent somewhere else. We have access to this field as illustrated by these experiments. Braden speculates that this field probably originated when creation did—with the Big Bang or whatever the beginning was. Braden writes, "The matrix of energy that explains why the three experiments work as they do also demonstrates how the positive feelings and prayers within us can be so effective in the world around us. The Divine Matrix is what *space itself* is made of. Wherever space exists there is also subtle energy. It's what fills the emptiness between you and the words you are reading."

This is significant as it helps us to understand how much power we have. Any change that we wish to see in our world—from healing for ourselves and our loved ones to peace in conflict areas—doesn't have to be *sent* from our hearts and minds anywhere. Our thoughts and prayers within us are already everywhere.

In addition to the divine matrix, Braden uses the concept of the hologram to explain how this works.

In a *hologram* every fragment, no matter how small, contains/reflects the whole. The original image of the whole is contained in all of its many parts. Any change made to one of those segments shows up everywhere throughout the hologram.

"The subtle power of the hologram is that it offers us the leverage to make a tremendous change on a large scale by altering a pattern in only one place. Nothing is local or limited to where and when it is happening" (Braden).

A single change in one place can make a difference everywhere.

***

The concept of an energy field or matrix that links everyone and everything also exists in the world of healing. David Cumes (a physician) believes in an energy field that he considers to be part of the healing process. "Not only are we in the Field but the Field is in us. The cosmic Field seems to extend from us as an energy reservoir in space through which signals pass back and forth."

Healers believe that it is possible to send healing energy to patients from a distance. Cumes quotes scientific evidence proving that messages and healing can be transmitted via the field. He also quotes an article by Fred Sicher from the *Western Journal of Medicine*, describing research involving AIDS patients. One group received psychic healing from afar over a period of two months, while the second group (the control) did not. To eliminate the possibility of a placebo effect, neither group knew who was getting the treatment. The mortality in the control group was 40 percent, but there were no deaths in the treatment group. In addition, the latter did significantly better regarding AIDS-defining diseases, number of hospitalizations and length of hospital stay, severity of depression and anxiety, and overall vigor. This effect has earned recognition from the National Institute of Health, which has termed it *distant mental influence on biological systems*.

The same holds for prayer, which has been shown to have beneficial effects on the sick. Many would explain improvements in health as the placebo effect. However, when patients are unaware that they are being prayed for, we can assume that the placebo effect is not involved. "Healing is such a mystery," says Cumes, who believes that the field and the divine Spirit assist in the process.

Could it be that the energy field of the healer is the same field that physicists describe? Science tells us that matter and space are inseparable and interdependent parts of a single whole. According to quantum mechanics, everything is connected at the subatomic level. The quantum field is seen as the fundamental physical entity—a continuous medium that is present everywhere in space.

When Einstein was asked about the nature of the cosmos, he said, "We know nothing about it at all. Our knowledge is but the knowledge of school children." When questioned about our knowledge of the cosmos in the future, he said, "Possibly we shall know a little more than we do now. But the real nature of things—that we shall never know, never."

***

Based on the scientific information described in this chapter, and chapter 5, we can summarize that *all is energy, everything in the universe is interconnected*, and *a small change in one place will trigger a change in other places.* This new understanding of our world has led scientists to believe that a *new vision of reality* is now occurring in science. There is a fundamental change of worldview taking place that has transformational implications for our culture and society at large (Capra).

We are all made of atoms, photons, and electrons, and we are in a constant state of vibration. We are made of the same stuff that originated with the Big Bang, and like atoms and subatomic particles, we remain interconnected irrespective of distance and time.

Quantum theory and the experiments described earlier in this chapter, support the notion that we are *participants* in all that happens in our world and not passive bystanders.

***

This very superficial and simplified discussion of the new science (written by a non-physicist for the layman) is presented here to demonstrate how concepts that once may have been regarded as absurd gradually become accepted as fact, as new discoveries are made and new theories are proposed. This is how scientific ideas change over time.

The new science, and quantum mechanics in particular, are bringing together the seen and the unseen to give us a new understanding of our world. This is leading to a convergence of science and spirituality as discussed in the next chapter.

Physics is the reality of the way things work, the reality you sit in.
God is the physicist.

—Kryon

Chapter 15

The Merging of Science and Mysticism

The most beautiful and profound emotion we can experience is the sensation of the mystical. It is the sower of all true science.

—Albert Einstein

The first book I read that compares science with the mysticism of the East was *The Tao of Physics* by Fritjof Capra, a researcher in high-energy physics. Capra's interest in Eastern mysticism led him to discover parallels between it and modern physics. He reached the conclusion that Eastern mysticism provides a consistent philosophical framework that can accommodate our most advanced theories of the physical world. "The two foundations of the twentieth century physics—quantum theory and relativity—both force us to see the world very much in the same way a Hindu, Buddhist or Taoist sees it."

In a form that the layman can understand, Capra gives eloquent descriptions of modern physics, Eastern mysticism, and the parallels between the two. The reluctance of modern scientists to accept the similarities between their concepts and those of mystics does not surprise him since mysticism—at least in the West—has traditionally been associated quite erroneously with things vague, mysterious, and highly unscientific. Fortunately, this attitude is changing. As Eastern thought has begun to interest a significant number of people and meditation is no longer viewed with ridicule or suspicion, mysticism is being taken seriously even within the scientific community.

The Tao of Physics was received with great enthusiasm in England and the United States. Though the book had only minimal promotion or advertising, it spread rapidly by word of mouth. It has been published in forty-three editions around the world and translated into twenty-three languages. This tremendous response from people from all walks of life demonstrates great empathy for Capra's views.

Capra concedes that the recognition of the similarities between modern physics and Eastern mysticism is part of a fundamental change of worldviews in science and society. There is a profound change of consciousness that many people have felt intuitively over the past two or three decades, and this is why Capra's book has struck such a responsive chord.

Of course, there has been criticism of *The Tao of Physics* because of a widespread misunderstanding of the nature of mysticism, which Capra explains as follows: In the scientific community, mysticism is generally thought of as something very vague, fuzzy, and highly unscientific. Naturally, physicists do not like to see their cherished theories being compared with this subject. "This erroneous view of mysticism is really very unfortunate, because when you look at the classic texts of mystical traditions, you will find that deep mystical experience is never described as vague or nebulous, but on the contrary, is always associated with clarity."

In the Eastern worldview, the constituents of matter and the basic phenomena involving them are all interconnected. The most important characteristic of Eastern mysticism is the awareness of the mutual interrelation of all things and events. All things are seen as interdependent and inseparable.

Quantum mechanics has lead scientists to realize that at the atomic level, nature comprises a network of relations, forming an interconnected web. The material world is a network of inseparable patterns of relationships. The planet as a whole is a living, self-regulating system, and humans are just one particular strand in the web of life.

Capra's understanding of the concept that everything is interconnected has been strengthened by his study of ecological systems, where all the components are interrelated and interdependent. Ecology brings us the awareness of being connected with all of nature. At this deep level, ecology merges with spirituality because the experience of being connected with all of nature and belonging to the universe is the very essence of spirituality. Capra describes "spiritual experience" as an experience of the unity of body and mind as well as a feeling of union between the self and the world—a profound sense of oneness with all, of belonging to the universe as a whole.

Man did not weave the web of life—he is merely a strand in it. Whatever he does to the web, he does to himself.

—Chief Seattle, Native American, 1854

In the mid-twentieth century, the physicists Niels Bohr and Werner Heisenberg emphasized the notion of quantum interconnectedness. They stated, "The new kind of interconnectedness that has recently emerged not only enforces the similarities between the views of physicists and mystics; it also raises the intriguing possibility of relating subatomic physics to Jungian psychology and, perhaps, even to parapsychology."

Heisenberg, a key pioneer of quantum mechanics, once admitted to Capra, "Learning about Indian philosophy confirms that the new ideas in quantum physics are not that crazy since there is a whole culture that subscribes to very similar ideas." His colleague Bohr (Nobel laureate in physics, 1922) reached the same conclusion after a visit to China.

Buddhist monk and Zen master Thich Nhat Hanh coined the term *interbeing*. It emphasizes the interrelationship and interdependence of all persons to one another and to all things. "Interbeing is not a theory; it is a reality that can be directly experienced by each of us at any moment in our daily lives."

The concept supports the Buddhist philosophy of nonviolence.

Do you ever feel sad or anxious for no apparent reason? There are times when I experience an overwhelming sadness that seems to enter by "osmosis". If quantum theory is correct and we are all connected, then it does not take a great stretch of the imagination to see that we are affected by the suffering of others. How can we remain untouched when millions of people all around us are the victims of war, are denied basic human rights, or are subjected to discrimination and repression? My thoughts go out to the migrant workers (many from the Far East) who move to other countries in order to earn money to support their families. Where I live, there are many such foreign workers—caregivers, construction workers, and farm helpers. They are conspicuous by virtue of their ethnic appearance, and yet they are invisible to most of us. We are oblivious of their loneliness and the hardships of living alone in a foreign land. Even in the "civilized" world, people in our midst are subjected to discrimination, humiliation, and the various kinds of violence that are widespread in modern society.

We are energy beings living in a universe of energy.
We change the energies within and around us with every thought,
every action, and every emotion.

—Joey Korn, spiritual dowser and author

***

Neurologist Eben Alexander, a man of science who for years rejected the notion of spirituality, reached a new understanding after a near-death experience. He says there is a huge chasm between our current scientific understanding of the universe and the truth as he now sees it. In his book *Proof of Heaven*, Alexander states, "In my past view, *spiritual* wasn't a word that I would have employed during a scientific conversation. Now I believe it is a word that we cannot afford to leave out."

Chapter 16

The Empowered Human Being

We create our reality through the choices we make, and it starts with our thoughts. What we think is what we manifest.

Sometimes it may be hard to admit that you create your reality. You may stop and ask yourself, "Did *I* create this?" Once you connect your actions to your choices, you can take responsibility for the way your life is going.

> Your mind is a garden, your thoughts are the seeds.
> You can grow flowers, or you can grow weeds.
>
> —Source unknown

In John Kehoe's book *Mind Power into the 21ˢᵗ Century*, which is filled with wisdom and guidance on self-empowerment, he writes, "Our normal thoughts can be compared to sparks from a fire. Though they contain the essence and potential power of the flame, they normally dissipate quickly. They last only a few seconds, fly into the air and quickly burn out. Weak and scattered thoughts are weak and scattered forces. Strong and concentrated thoughts are strong and concentrated forces."

Through repetition, the power of a thought can be magnified and is more readily able to manifest itself.

The subconscious is the mechanism through which conscious thought-impulses that are repeated regularly are changed into their physical equivalent. You can voluntarily plant in your subconscious mind any plan, thought, or purpose that you desire to translate into its physical counterpart, and it will manifest itself for you. The subconscious is ever-ready to serve you, yet so few of us understand how to use its power.

Kehoe explains how the conscious and subconscious minds work together as a team to create our reality. He uses the following analogy: "Your subconscious mind is like fertile soil that accepts any seed you plant within it. Your habitual thoughts and beliefs are the seeds which are being constantly sown within, and they produce in your life what is planted just as surely as corn kernels produce corn. You will reap what you sow. This is a law. Remember, the conscious mind is the gardener. It is our responsibility to be aware of and choose wisely what reaches the inner garden."

It is very important to point out here that your subconscious mind is not judgmental. It does not choose which thoughts to act upon. So if you "feed" it nonbeneficial ideas through negative thoughts (via your conscious mind), it will manifest these.

In his book *The Silva Mind Control Method*, Jose Silva teaches how to improve one's life by using the power of the mind. He gives practical, logical methods that are actually quite simple based on the same principles about the subconscious mind as described in this chapter.

Silva's book may seem dated as it was written in 1977, but like all solid principles, his teachings remain relevant to this day. It instructs you on how you can effectively heal your body and solve problems through meditation, creative visualization, and affirmations. In short, it teaches how to improve your life by using your mind, but like all good techniques, they must be put into practice and not left on the printed page.

Both of the previously mentioned authors teach the techniques described in the following sections, which can be found in the writings of many other authors and great thinkers:

Affirmation and Visualization

Affirmations are simple statements repeated to yourself silently or aloud, whatever feels most comfortable and practical to you at the time. You can do them anywhere. You decide upon a statement that represents what you want to have happen to you, and you repeat it to yourself over and over again. Affirmations should be short and simple and easy to repeat. Always affirm in the positive. For example, if you want to reduce your consumption of food, you wouldn't say, "I'm not going to overeat." According to Kryon, the most effective way to use affirmations is to say them as if what you desire is happening now and not at some future moment. For example, you would say, "I am healthy. I am joyful."

Visualization is a technique in which you picture in your mind what you want to have happen. The technique is amazingly effective, and it is described in other well-known publications. Shakti Gawain, who wrote *Creative Visualization*, teaches you how to relax deeply and then picture a desired goal in your mind exactly the way you want it to be. It works by the law of attraction through which the thought frequencies that we send out merge with matching frequencies around us. In this way you attract to yourself that which you desire. (see The Teachings of Abraham in chapter 13). The book *The Secret*, a best seller written by Byrne Rhonda, is based on this technique. Kehoe teaches how to enhance the process by adding feelings to the pictures in our visualizations. In other words, *feel* the success of whatever event you are visualizing—e.g., feel the accomplishment as you visualize yourself giving a highly successful presentation at work.

There are numerous reports of the efficacy of these techniques in the literature. A well-known affirmation that was taught decades ago to cure illnesses by the pioneer of affirmation techniques Emile Coue is widely used to this day: *Every day in every way, I am getting better and better.* Coue told his patients to repeat this affirmation every morning upon arising and every evening before going to sleep for two minutes each time. The effect was so dramatic that he wrote several books on the subject of self-suggestion and taught people around the world the curative properties of the mind when directed toward recovery. Emile Coue is credited with the documented cures of thousands of people.

The first step to a more successful life is incredibly easy. Pay attention to your thoughts and consciously create thoughts that match what you desire.

In his book *The Biology of Belief,* Bruce Lipton offers empowering information through his understanding that we are the creators of our lives and the world in which we live, thus replacing the belief that we are frail biochemical machines controlled by genes. This book has become notorious because it illuminates the self-limiting nature of negative beliefs. Lipton encourages us to take back control of our lives by changing beliefs that weaken us. We have the power within us. We just have to be aware of this and learn how to use it. "As we all know, knowledge is power and consequently knowledge of self provides self-empowerment," says Lipton.

***

It would be wise to heed the advice of Zen master Thich Naht Hanh. He tells us that mindfulness is a useful tool to take you out of autopilot mode and bring you back to the here and now. Mindful meditation enables us to bring mind and body together, to be present, and to choose to respond appropriately in difficult situations rather than react automatically. Mindless reactions are often not in our best interest. *Stopping and calming ourselves* enables us to access our intuition and gain insight.

At times we may think that what we need most is peace of mind, and we may even achieve it. Then we hear bad news—a business deal fell through, the house was burgled, or a partner is being unfaithful. Suddenly, we find ourselves in the grip of anxiety. There may be anger as well. In an instant, peace of mind is forgotten, and something else is more important. In my case, discovering that my driver's license or credit card is missing, throws me into a spin.

To attain the equanimity of mind, which is the goal of most of the teachings mentioned, we need to take time to be still, to practice *intentional solitude*.

"Intentional solitude is the cure for the frazzled state so common to modern women, the one that makes her *ride in all directions*." These words come from Clarissa Pinkola Estes's book *Women Who Run with the Wolves*, and of course, they hold true for men as well. I love this book because it reveals a deep understanding of a woman's soul journey. Estes writes that women from ancient times as well as modern aboriginal women often set aside a sacred place—a certain tree, a place at the water's edge, a forest, or a quiet room—to listen to the inner self, to solicit advice and guidance otherwise impossible to hear in the din of daily life. "You need to take enough time away to revivify and renew yourself. Women tend not to understand *soul* as the central generator of their animation and energy. They treat their soul as if it were a not very important instrument." Like any instrument of value, the soul needs shelter and repair, otherwise the relationship sludges up and causes deceleration in a woman's life. Finally, it breaks down, out on heartbreak ridge. "Then, it is a long, long walk back home."

Taking time out for intentional solitude is like going home. "Home is an internal place. Home is where a thought or feeling can be sustained instead of being interrupted or torn away from us because something else is demanding our time or attention. It relates to time rather than space. The vehicles through which women reach home are many: music, art, forest, ocean, sunrise, solitude. These all take us home to a nutritive inner world" (Estes).

"The only thing one needs for intentional solitude is the ability to tune out distractions—from other people, from noise, from duties and work waiting to be done. During this time we bring all aspects of life to bear at one point, to assess: habit, work, creative life, mother/father, mate, children, sexuality, spiritual life. The measurement used in assessment is simple: What needs less? What needs more? What needs adjustment, work, or protection? What should you dispose of, move, change?"

This empowering process applies to all of us. We all need to return *home*.

Like scientist and author Bruce Lipton, perhaps some of us need a tune-up. He was going through life willy-nilly, mindlessly expending energy. By carefully examining where he was wasting his energy, he was able to get rid of activities like the deadly faculty parties that he didn't even enjoy. But he says, "It was harder to get rid of the energy-draining defeatist thinking in which I habitually engaged."

Again, it boils down to our thoughts.

***

Come to the edge.
We might fall
Come to the edge.
It's too high.
Come to the edge!
And they came,
and he pushed,
And they flew.

—Christopher Logue, contemporary poet

"With these words we are shown a beautiful example of the power that awaits us when we allow ourselves to venture beyond the bounds of what we've always believed to be true in our lives. It is in unchartered territory that we experience ourselves in a new way, and discover a new freedom" (Gregg Braden, referring to the above poem).

You can fly, but walking is comfortable—
so most will want to continue walking.

—Kryon

***

Coming at us from all directions is a wealth of new knowledge—both scientific and spiritual. Much of the current scientific discourse and the literature being published bring spirituality into scientific discussions. It is available for us to use it to rewrite the scripts of our lives.

Each one of us is a work in progress. Each person is in a continuous state of change. The world is changing. There is a new awareness, a recognition that some things are spiraling downward—our economic systems, governments, society. More than ever before, cases of bad management and bad government are coming to light thanks to investigative reporting by the media as well as the Internet and the transparency it provides. Corruption, greed and inefficiency in high places are being exposed. People are less prepared to tolerate the poor behavior of their leaders or the deception of large corporations.

There are signs that a shift in consciousness is occurring. Many present-day leaders are reluctant to become involved in foreign conflicts in contrast to the historical eagerness to engage in war. In Japan, the constitution outlaws involvement in war! Some leaders have apologized for the atrocities committed against whole populations in the past. Young people are talking to one another on social media across borders, getting to know and understand that the *other* has feelings and desires very similar to his own.

Recent popes have apologized repeatedly for the centuries-long horrors committed against Jews and others professing different faiths—in fact anyone who dared to voice beliefs that were different from those of the church. The current pope, Francis, a man of wisdom and compassion, is dismantling age-old barriers between religions. He literally embraces people of all traditions and social status. He brings people together instead of excluding and degrading those who have different beliefs. Just as the new science tells us, *we are all one, and we are all connected.*

Our guides and friends in the spirit world who bring us their teachings about life, death, and our rich spiritual heritage are gradually revealing what has mostly been "hidden." They tell us that we are developing a higher level of consciousness and are now ready to receive, understand, and accept information that has always been there behind the scenes. We have free choice either to reject this information or to open our minds and hearts to it. In our awakened state, we can easily absorb these teachings, sharpen our intuition, and claim our personal power.

Chapter 17

Closing Words

The purpose of this book is to share the information and wisdom that I have accumulated from many different sources and to bring awareness to tools that enhance our lives and well-being. Many different topics are covered. Each topic is vast, and I can give the reader only a *taste* of each one and the means (via the references) to delve deeper into the subjects that arouse his interest. Hopefully, this information will provide a useful starting point for readers to begin their own study of the holistic approach to well-being that includes spirit as well. It is a route to a more fulfilling life.

Many of the great minds of our time are expressing their belief that we create our own reality by interacting with the energy field in which we live. I have cited many authors' ideas regarding our connection to this field, to one another, and to Spirit. This world of ours is a living, vibrant system of energy. Every thought you think impresses itself upon this system. Whether you like it or not, you are forever creating your reality through what you are thinking.

So many people of wisdom tell us that our thoughts and imagination are the most powerful tools we have right here within ourselves. Visualization, affirmations, and intuition are practical tools that empower us to live the lives we want. To work with mind power, we do not have to understand how it works just as we don't have to understand how spark plugs fire in order to drive a car. Few of us understand automotive mechanics, but that doesn't stop us from driving. Likewise, in the science of mind power, anyone can quickly and successfully master the basics and effectively put them to work in his or her life.

We are living in a time of accelerated advancement in human consciousness. How consciousness and the physical world interact is now much less of a mystery to those who consider consciousness to be energy in its finest and most dynamic form. Authors such as Kehoe, Kuntz, Lipton, Braden and others believe that prayer and intuition are not supernatural phenomena but that they follow laws that we can use. What we visualize, want, or fear in the mind can be made real.

A Japanese scientist and doctor of alternative medicine, Masaru Emoto (1943–2014), made an amazing discovery. In the course of his research into the wave fluctuations in water, he began to take photographs of frozen ice crystals. He found that water from clear springs formed colorful, complex snowflake-like crystals while polluted water formed incomplete, asymmetrical patterns with dull colors. His research led him to the discovery that water exposed to different human thoughts and emotions displayed crystals of different formations. Loving or appreciative thoughts that were directed to the water produced beautiful, perfect crystals. Water exposed to thoughts of anger or hatred produced crystals that were deformed with incomplete, asymmetrical patterns.

Dr. Emoto began to photograph the different types of water crystals. In 1999, he self-published his photographs in a small Japanese book that was not intended to be sold in the large bookstores. However, through word of mouth, it became a best seller. After it was translated into English, Emoto began to receive requests from abroad to give lectures about his work. The people who attended his lectures and saw his photographs were deeply moved. I quote one person's response from Emoto's book *The Hidden Messages in Water*, "Through the photographs, I could see that the energy of our consciousness and words can change things that we can actually see with our eyes. This is the first and only way that this elusive energy can be viewed. We don't believe what we can't see, but the ice crystals show us everything."

Emoto explains the phenomenon of water reflecting what is in a person's mind and soul in terms of energy and vibration. "The entire universe is in a state of vibration, and each thing generates its own frequency … Human beings are also vibrating, and each individual vibrates at a unique frequency." A sad person will emit a sadness frequency, and a person experiencing joy will emit a corresponding frequency.

Thoughts and sound (in the form of spoken words) are vibrations and have an impact on the physical world around us as demonstrated by the experiments of Emoto with water. His work verifies the age-old idea of *mind over matter*.

***

Despite the pockets of "darkness" on the planet, there is an awakening taking place among people of all walks of life. More people than ever before are seeking spirituality. Our connection to the world of spirit provides us with a bridge to profound wisdom. Kryon tells us that only one half of 1 percent of the world population has to "awaken" in a certain way in order to effect a positive shift for the better on the planet. "The light of the few will illuminate things that were formerly in the dark. Profound change will occur. Leaderships will change. Refreshing ideas will emerge within governments that nobody ever thought of in the past."

This may seem impossible, but consider the change in behavior that was reported during a study done in Japan known as the "*hundredth monkey phenomenon.*"

In 1952, Japanese scientists were studying the behavior of wild macaque monkeys living on an island. The main food of the monkeys was a specific kind of root, which they dug out of the ground. One day the scientists noticed one of the monkeys doing something new. He washed the root before eating it. He repeated this on subsequent days, and gradually, other monkeys began to wash their food before eating it. After some time most of the monkeys on the island had adopted the new behavior. A few years later people on a nearby island began reporting that the monkeys on their island had started to wash their food. There had been no transfer of monkeys between the islands and no physical contact between them.

This story was first published in the West in the 1970s in the writings of Lyall Watson. It may be an amusing story because it involves a bunch of monkeys, but it supports the theory that a new idea or behavior can spread in an unexplained way once a critical number of individuals have adopted it. I want to point out that the majority of monkeys that picked up the new behavior were juveniles. Many of the adults did not.

The hundredth monkey phenomenon has become popular as it demonstrates the potential for social change. It also supports the concept of the collective unconscious proposed by Carl Jung.

If we apply this concept to human society, could it indicate that a change for the better in the world is largely dependent on the younger generation? It may be, but the older generation should not feel helpless to effect positive change since the behavior of each one of us can have a significant effect.

How did the information pass from island to island without physical contact between the communities?

Gawain explains it as follows: "Every individual's consciousness is connected to, and is part of the mass consciousness. When a small but significant number of individuals have moved into a new level of awareness and significantly changed their behavior, that change is felt in the entire mass consciousness. Other individuals are then moved in the direction of that change."

Peace activists are validating this concept. With the aid of the Internet, they are holding global synchronized meditations for peace. James Twyman (www.jamestwyman.com), William Rand (www.reiki.org/wpcm.html), Barbara Wolf (www.globalmeditations.com), and others individually mobilize thousands of people across the world to meditate or pray together for peace. They are showing that "focused, affirmative prayer has the ability to shift crime rates, terrorist attacks, and even wars" (Twyman).

Dr. Richard Gerber recalls the research that was carried out on transcendental meditation (TM). When large groups of people meditated in major cities, crime rates dropped dramatically. The crime rates in those cities rose again after the meditators left. Gerber concludes, "The implication is that the energy fields of the meditators had calming, peaceful effects upon the city dwellers."

Gerber refers to the work of Ilya Prigogine, who won the Nobel Prize for his theory of dissipative structures. This theory suggests that if enough key components of a system are shifted into a new energy state, then this critical mass can catapult the whole system into a new energetic equilibrium. Relating this idea to the TM research, Gerber postulates that meditating together in peace and love created an effect that was able to shift the equilibrium of the whole system. The meditators' healing intent caused energetic changes in the population of the cities involved. This ripple of peace and tranquility shifted the chaotic equilibrium of life toward a slightly more peaceful state, which lasted for the few days or weeks that the meditation groups met.

Kryon explains it in terms of the new science, "Quantum energy is everywhere all the time and reacts to other quantum energy with the rules of quantum energy."

This concept is supported by the ideas discussed in chapter 14, "The New Science." Scientist Gregg Braden believes that there is a field that he calls the Divine Matrix, which connects everyone and everything in the universe and accounts for the quantum effects we observe in the experiments described in the previously mentioned chapter. Furthermore, Braden uses the concept of the holographic universe to demonstrate how a change on any level is reflected throughout the whole. Thus, he says that it doesn't take many people to anchor a new way of thinking or believing within the overall pattern of consciousness.

We are still a little *green* when it comes to understanding this, and Kryon compares our present stage with the following scenario: Imagine telling people living less than two hundred years ago that one day we would throw voices and moving pictures through the air and the entire world would hear and see them instantly. They would not believe it, and we would be considered unbalanced. "How do you explain the Internet to someone who doesn't know about electricity yet? Where do you begin? This is the issue today."

Kryon tells us that the present trend is pointing to the potential for a new world with a higher consciousness and more integrity, and proclaims that he came in order to accelerate this change. Kryon foresees a future with a humanity that has matured to become more *balanced*, *compassionate*, and *tolerant*.

The word *compassion* appears many times throughout this book. In the words of Zen master Thich Nhat Hanh, compassion means literally "to suffer with, to recognize the suffering of the other through the ability to put oneself in his skin, and to attempt to remove that suffering."

We are all connected—through the field of consciousness and quantum energy that is our reality. "Together we create the healing or the suffering, the peace or the war. This could very well be the most difficult implication of what the new science is showing us. And it might also be the source of our greatest healing and survival" (Braden).

We are all made of the same "stuff", and since we are connected to one another and to the earth, it follows that when a person or our planet is harmed, we are *all* harmed in some way.

Often we feel helpless in the face of the sad state of our world. At such moments it is worth remembering the concept that *only a small percentage of the whole* is needed to bring about a dynamic shift of the whole system. Therefore, any effort to bring peace and light to our fellow man at a personal level contributes to a shift on the planet as a whole.

Each one of us can contribute to the creation of a better world.

***

Whole fields of study exist for *each* concept touched upon in this book. Any one book can deal only with a fraction of the available information in the present world of rapidly expanding knowledge. So many facts are known, and many different interpretations emerge around these facts. Even our fundamental notion of reality is up for debate, thanks to new discoveries and technologies that drive scientific thought and produce new ideas.

We have free choice to embrace the beliefs that best suit our personal nature and to adopt the tools that can help us to live the lives we want. We are limited only by our thinking.

Our thoughts and emotions are transmitted instantly and continuously through an energy field that connects everything and everyone. By projecting thoughts of compassion, brotherhood, tolerance, and healing, we can make this world a better place. Remember, a small number of people shining their light can bring about change that benefits all of humanity.

Acknowledgments

My thanks go to Ellinor Lips for the excellent work she did in proofreading the manuscript; to Ina Friedman for her professional opinion about the text; to Miriam Klein Sofer for her patience when editing and providing technical assistance to finalize the manuscript for submission. Thank you to Ami Perach for his encouragement and for providing a quiet space in a beautiful setting for a number of weeks, where I could write undisturbed; And I'd like to thank my coffee buddies who never complained when I didn't have time for them because I had to "work on my book".

Special thanks go to Balboa Press for their constant assistance throughout the publishing process. Their communications with me were always supportive and pleasant.

A sincere thanks to all the authors that are cited in the book for sharing their knowledge and insights and for inspiring all of us. Last but definitely not least— to Kryon, Abraham, Veronica, Orin, Daben, and others like them as well as their wonderful human channelers, for bringing us their teachings from the other side, always given with love.

Bibliography

Aesoph, Lauri M. *How to Eat Away Arthritis*. New York: Prentice Hall Press (revised and expanded ed.), 1996.

Agatston, Arthur. *The South Beach Diet Gluten Solution*. New York: Rodale, 2013.

Alexander, Eben. *Proof of Heaven. A Neurosurgeon's Journey into the Afterlife*. New York: Simon & Schuster, 2012.

Balch, Phyllis A. *Prescription for Nutritional Healing*. New York: Avery (Penguin Group), 2006.

Bays, Brandon. *The Journey*. New York: Atria Paperback (Simon & Schuster), revised edition, 2012.

Borysenko, Joan. www.joanborysenko.com

Braden, Gregg. *The Isaiah Effect: Decoding the Lost Science of Prayer and Prophecy*. New York: Three Rivers Press (Random House, Inc.), 2000.

Braden, Gregg. *The Divine Matrix: Bridging Time, Space, Miracles and Belief*. New York: Hay House, Inc., 2007.

Brennan, Barbara Ann. *Hands of Light. A Guide to Healing Through the Human Energy Field*. New York: Bantom Books,1988.

Brennan, Barbara Ann. *Light Emerging. The Journey of Personal Healing*. New York: Bantom Books, 1993.

Byrne Rhonda. *The Secret*. New York: Simon & Schuster, 2006.

Canadian Government. Report title: Oxirane, (chloromethyl)-(Epichlorohydrin). www.chemicalsubstances.gc.ca

Capra, Fritjof. *The Tao of Physics* (Fifth Edition). Boston, MA: Shambhala Publications, Inc., 2010.

Carroll, Lee, a channeler for Kryon and author of the Kryon Books (seventeen in number). New York: The Kryon Writings, Inc., 1993–2017.

Carter, Midred, and Tammy Weber. *Body Reflexology: Healing at Your Fingertips*. Revised and updated edition. Eaglewood Cliffs, NJ: Prentice Hall, 1994.

Chan, Pedro. *Finger Acupressure: Treatment for Many Common Ailments*. New York: Ballantine Books, 1974.

Chapman, Gary. *The 5 Love Languages. The Secret to Love That Lasts.* Chicago, IL: Northfirld Publishing, 1992.

Chevalier, Gaetan. *The Physics of Earthing—Simplified*. Article in Ober et al, 2014, pp. 255-265.

Childers, Dr. Norman. http://www.noarthritis.com/nightshades.htm.

Church, Dawson. *The Genie in Your Genes.* Epigenetic Medicine andf the New Biology. Santa Rosa, CA: Elite Books, 2007.

Clark, Glenn. *The Man who Tapped the Secrets of the Universe*. Mansfield Centre, CT: Matino Publishing, Mansfield Center, 2011.

Coelho, Paulo. *The Alchemist.* New York: HarperCollins Publishers, 1995.

Crawford, April. A deep trance medium who channels the spirit guide Veronica. www.AprilCrawford.com.

Crawford, April and Veronica. *Heavenly Match*. La Crescenta, CA, Connecting Wave, 2014.

Cumes, David. *The Spirit of Healing*. St. Paul, MN: Llewellyn Publications, 1999.

Davis, Adelle. *Let's Get Well*. New York: Signet, New American Library, 1965.

Davis, Adelle. *Let's Eat Right To Keep Fit*. New York: Signet, New American Library, 1970.

Davis, William. *Wheat Belly. Lose the Wheat Lose the Weight, and Find Your Path Back to Health*. New York: Rodale, 2011.

Dennison, Paul. *Brain Gym and Me*. Ventura, CA: Edu-Kinestics, Inc., 2006.

Edward, John. *Infinite Quest. Develop your Psychic Intuition and take Charge of Your Life*. New York/London: Sterling, 2010.

Emoto, Masaru. *The Hidden Messages in Water*. New York: Atria Books (Simon & Schuster, Inc.), 2004.

Estes, Clarissa Pinkola. *Women Who Run with the Wolves*. New York: Ballantine Books, 1992.

Fenwick, Elizabeth, and Tony Smith. *Adolescence: The Survival Guide for Parents and Teenagers*. London: Dorling Kindersley, 1994.

Fisher, Joe. *The Case for Reincarnation*. London: Diamond Books, 1984.

Ford, Arthur. *The Life Beyond Death*. London: Sphere Books, 1974.

Freed, Jeffrey, and Laurie Parsons. *Right-Brained Children in a Left-Brained World*. New York: Simon & Schuster Paperbacks, 1997.

Gawain, Shakti, and Laurel King. *Living in the Light*. Ashland, OR: The Pythagorean Press, 1986.

Gerber, Richard. *Vibrational Medicine. The #1 Handbook of Subtle-Energy Therapies*, 3rd ed. Rochester, VT: Bear and Company, 2001.

Gilbert, Elizabeth. *Eat, Pray, Love*. New York: Riverhead Books, 2006.

Gibran, Kahlil. *The Prophet*. New York: Alfred A. Knopf, Inc., 1923.

Glasser, Howard, and Jennifer Easley. *Transforming the Difficult Child. A Nurtured Heart Approach*. Alberton, South Africa: Lourie Publishing (Pty) Ltd, 1999.

Hannaford, Carla. *Smart Moves. Why Learning Is Not All In Your Head*, 2nd ed. Salt Lake City, UT: Great River Books, 2005.

Hawking, Stephen, and Leonard Mlodinow. *The Grand Design*. London: Bantam Books, 2010.

Hawksley, Lucinda, and Ian Whitelaw (Editors). *101 Essential Tips—YOGA*. London: Dorling Kindersley Limited, 1995.

Hicks, Esther, and Jerry Hicks. *Ask and It Is Given*. New York: Hay House, 2004.

Honervogt, Tanmaya. *The Power of Reiki*. New York: Henry Holt and Company Inc., 1998.

Hutchinson, Ronald. *YOGA: A Way of Life*. London: Hamlyn, 1974.

Jensen, Frances E. *The Teenage Brain. A Neuroscientist's Survival Guide to Raising Adolescents and Young Adults*. London: Thorsons, 2015.

Ju-Li, Wang. *Chinese Channel Theory*. https://www.eastlandpress.com/upload/0-939616-6_pdf_excerpt_20080418184708_1/act.pdf.

Kabat-Zinn, Jon. *Wherever You Go, There You Are*. New York: Hyperion, 1994.

Kehoe, John. *Mind Power into the 21st Century*, 10th Anniversary ed. Vancouver, Canada: Zoetic Inc., 1996.

Keleman, Lawrence. *To Kindle a Soul*. Southfield, MI: Targum Press Inc., 2001.

Keogh, Justin, Andrew Kilding, Phillipa Pidgeon, Linda Ashley, and Dawn Gillis. "Physical Benefits of Dancing for Healthy Older Adults: A Review." *Journal of Aging and Physical Activity* 17: 1–23 (2009).

Kindlon, Dan, and Michael Thompson. *Raising Cain. Protecting the Emotional Life of Boys*. New York: Random House, 2000.

Korn, Joey. *Dowsing: A Path to Enlightenment*. Augusta,GA: New Millennium Press, 1997.

Kryon, a divine messenger who brings us teachings from the other side, by channeling information through Lee Carroll. These channelings (from 1987 to the present day) can be found at www.kryon.com, either as transcriptions or in audio form.

Kubler-Ross, Elizabeth. *On Death and Dying*. London: Macmillan Publishing Company, 1969.

Kubler-Ross Elizabeth. *The Wheel of Life. A memoir of Living and Dying*. London: Toronto, Bantam Press, 1997.

Kubler-Ross, Elizabeth, and David Kessler. *Life Lessons*. New York: Simon & Schuster, 2002.

Kuntz, Ted. *Peace Begins With Me.* British Columbia, Canada: 2005.

Kushner, Harold. *Who Needs God.* New York: Simon and Schuster, 1989.

Lipton, Bruce. *The Biology of Belief.* Santa Rosa, CA: Elite Books, 2005.

Lustig, Robert. *Fat Chance: Beating the Odds Against Sugar, Processed Food, Obesity and Disease.* London: Fourth Estate, 2014.

McLaughlin, Chris, and Nicola Hall. *Secrets of Reflexology.* London: Dorling Kindersley, 2001.

Mercola, Joseph. Plastic and Cancerous Compounds in Tea Bags—A Surprising Source of Potential Toxins: http://articles.mercola.com/sites/articles/archive/2013/04/24/tea-bags.aspx.

Moody, Raymond. *Life After Life.* Internet Open Library, Mockingbird Books, Inc., 1975.

Murphy, Joseph. *The Power of Your Subconscious Mind.* New York: Bantam, 1982.

Narada, Maha Thera. *The Buddha and His Teachings.* Taipei, Taiwan: The Corporate Body of the Buddha Dharma Education Association, Inc., 1964.

Nelson, David, and Michael Cox. *Lehninger Principles of Biochemistry.* New York: Freeman & Company, 2005.

Norman, Laura. *Feet First: A Guide to Foot Reflexology.* New York: Simon & Schuster, 1988

Norris, Chuck. *The Secret Power Within: Zen Solutions to Real Problems.* New York: Broadway Books, 1996.

Null, Gary, Carolyn Dean, Martin Feldman, Debora Rasio, and Dorothy Smith. *Death by Medicine.* Mount Jackson, VA: Praktikos Books, 2011.

Ober, Clinton, Stephen Sinatra, and Martin Zucker. *Earthing—The Most Important Health Discovery Ever!* 2nd ed. Laguna Beach, CA: Basic Health Publications, Inc., 2014.

Orin and Daben, spirit guides channeled through Sanaya Roman and Duane Packer respectively. See the reference Roman and Packer, 1987.

Pearl, Eric. *The Reconnection*. Carlsbad, CA: Hay House, Inc., 2001.

Perlmutter, David. *Grain Brain*. New York: Little Brown and Company (Hachette Book Group), 2013.

Pike, James, and Dianne Kennedy. *The Other Side: An Account of My Experiences with Psychic Phenomena*. New York: Doubleday, 1968.

Roman, Sanaya, and Duane Packer. *Opening to Channel: How to Connect with Your Guide.* Tiburon, CA: HJ Kramer Inc., 1987.

Schucman, Helen. *A Course in Miracles*. New York: The Foundation for Inner Peace, 1976.

Silva, Jose. *The Silva Mind Control Method*. New York: Simon & Schuster, Inc., 1977.

Silverberg, Donald. "Pole Walking—Step in the Right Direction." *ESRA Magazine* 182: 56–58 (Dec. 2015/Jan. 2016).

Swain, Jasper. *Heaven's Gift*. Fish Hoek, South Africa: Kima Global Publishers, 1996.

Thick Nhat Hanh. *Old Path White Clouds: Walking in the Footsteps of the Buddha.* Berkeley, CA: Parallax Press, 1991.

Thick Nhat Hanh. *The Heart of the Buddha's Teaching. Transforming Suffering into Peace, Joy, and Liberation*. New York: Broadway Books, 1998.

Thie, John, and Matthew Thie. *Touch for Health. A Practical Guide to Natural Health with Acupressure Touch*. Camarillo, CA: DeVorss Publications, 2005.

Thomson, Janet. *Tapping for Life.* New York: Hay House, 2010.

Thompson, William Forde, and Gottfried Schlaug. "The Healing Power of Music." *Scientific American MIND* 26 (2): 32–41 (March/April 2015).

Tibika, Françoise. *Molecular Consciousness: Why the Universe Is Aware of Our Presence*. Rochester, VT: Park Street Press, 2010.

Tolle, Eckhart. *A New Earth: Awakening to Your Life's Purpose.* New York: Penguin Books, 2005.

Van Praagh, James. *Heaven and Earth: Making the Psychic Connection.* London:Ryder, 2001.

Veronica, a spirit guide who speaks and writes through April Crawford, a deep trance medium. www.AprilCrawford.com ; http://innerwhispers.net

Von Baeyer, Hans Christian. "Quantum Weirdness? It's All in Your Mind." *Scientific American special edition, Physics at the Limits* 1: 92–97 (November 4, 2015).

Weiss, Brian. *Many Lives, Many Masters.* New York: Simon & Schuster, 1988.

Weiss, Brian. *Miracles Happen. The Transformational Healing Power of Past Life Memories.* New York: HarperCollins Publishers, 2012.

Williams, Mark, and Danny Penman. *Mindfulness—A Practical Guide to Finding Peace in a Frantic World.* London: Piatkus, 2011.

Williamson, Marrianne. *A Return to Love: Reflections on the Principles of A Course in Miracles.* New York: HarperPerennial, 1993.

Wright, Janet. *Reflexology and Acupressure.* London: Hamlyn, 2008.

Printed in the United States
By Bookmasters